Aikido

The Contemporary Martial Art of Harmony
Training Methods and Spiritual Teachings

Moriteru Ueshiba
Doshu of Aikido

JN226067

Naigai Publishing Co.LTD

2-1-11 Higashiueno
 Taito-ku Tokyo, Japan 110-8578
Telephone ✚ 81-3-5830-0368
Facsimile ✚ 81-3-5830-0378
https://www.naigai-p.co.jp
ISBN 978-4-86257-472-5
Printed in Japan

Aikido, the Contemporary Martial Art of Harmony:
Training Methods and Spiritual Teachings

Moriteru Ueshiba
Doshu of Aikido

Translated by
Yoshifumi Saito

Contents

Preface *7*

History of Aikido *11*

Training Methods and Spiritual Teachings of Aikido *45*

Tradition of Aikido *139*

Preface

It was in 1957 (the 32nd year of the Showa era) that Kisshomaru Ueshiba, my father and the second Doshu [Leader] of aikido, wrote *Aikido* (published by Kowado), the first aikido-related book ever published after the war, in the hope of spreading the methods and teachings of aikido to the general public. In those days aikido was practiced behind closed doors and acknowledged only by a small number of people as a mysterious martial art created by Morihei Ueshiba, my grandfather and the Founder [*Kaiso*] of aikido. It was normal practice before and during the war that budo students, including our Founder's, simply observed and learned the skills of their respective masters, who did not make any logical explanations about them. The Founder did give some explanations concerning the spirit of aikido, which, however, were extremely difficult even for his immediate disciples to understand with a lot of references to *Kojiki* [Records of Ancient Matters] or *kotodama* [the soul of language]. The book *Aikido*, in which my father systematically and logically explained the skills and moves of aikido and translated the Founder's words into generally understandable ones, provided the teaching standards of aikido, which had already been widely practiced in post-war Japan, thereby playing an important role in attracting a growing number of incoming students.

After that my father kept publishing books on the methodology and spirit of aikido. In 1981 he published *Aikido no Kokoro* [The Spirit of Aikido], where he explained the spirit of aikido in plain language to meet the demands of wider and varied audience of the times both inside and outside Japan. This book was translated into foreign languages and became an international best-seller read by aikido students all over the world.

Thirty-seven years have passed since the publication of the book, and nearly twenty years since the death of my father in 1999 (the 11th year of the Heisei era). Aikido, having been more popularized, is now practiced in one hundred and forty countries and regions in the world, and there are two thousand and four hundred Aikikai-affiliated dojos, clubs, and organizations in Japan. In this new situation of unprecedented expansion of the aikido circle, I have found it necessary, as the present Doshu, to rephrase the teachings concerning the very core of aikido, that is to say, the methodology of 'training' and the 'spirit' beneath it, so that they may suit modern times. This is why I have decided to write this book.

I have neither studied *Kojiki* or *kotodama* like the Founder nor learned their meanings from him. Nevertheless, I know how my father understood the Founder's ideals and devoted his entire life to the popularization and promotion of aikido. I grew up seeing my father teach every morning class and supervise training sessions in the dojo and always tried my best to practice aikido for forty-six years since taking my first substantial lesson. I think I understand better than anybody else what the Founder and Kisshomaru the second Doshu had in mind when they tried to convey the ideals of aikido to the general public.

I tried my best to write this book in such plain language that even beginners can understand easily. Even in that plain language, I hope, the essence of aikido that the Founder and Kisshomaru the second Doshu tried to convey to the world will present itself to the reader. It is my earnest desire that this book will enrich every aikido student's daily training and also encourage those who have not practiced aikido to start learning it.

History of Aikido

Accumulation of Small Things

After the war, in the early 20th of the Showa era, my father (Kisshomaru Ueshiba, the second Doshu of aikido) resumed aikido training in Tokyo and, in 1956 (the 31st year of the Showa period), had an early retirement from Osaka Trading Company [the predecessor of Mizuho Securities Co., Ltd.] to specialize in teaching aikido. Some sixty years have passed after that, and now aikido is practiced enthusiastically in one hundred and forty countries and regions in the world, and in Japan there are two thousand and four hundred affiliated dojos and organizations, including clubs in universities and classes in adult education schools.

When aikido started to be popularized, its reputation spread among people, quite often embellished with episodes of 'the dojo of death in Ushigome' where great aikidoists—Morihei Ueshiba the venerable Founder of aikido, to start with, who was my grandfather with a strong personality and peerless genius of martial arts, and live-in disciples from the prewar period—applied themselves to hard training every day. Now that we have an increasing number of trainees and people engaged in aikido-related activities, we can neither represent aikido nor discuss its history through those episodes. I firmly believe that the history of aikido and that of Aikikai have been made by all its trainees; that aikido today has been made possible based on the collective efforts they have untiringly made in everyday training.

Born into the Ueshiba family, the head family of aikido, and bred in the house contiguous to the Hombu [Head] Dojo, I used to look upon the process of aikido getting more and more popular as the course of nature, while understanding how hard my grandfather and father worked and what kind of job I was to take over. After getting professionally engaged in aikido, I learned a lot from the way my father worked as the Doshu of aikido and chief director of the Aikikai Foundation, sometimes helping him with his work, and have worked myself as hard as possible for the popularization and promotion of aikido. Now that I can no longer learn from my father, I am determined to go forward, letting my son learn from me.

In retrospect, I find a variety of factors that have made aikido prevail so widely. On the other hand, I can find no specific promotional activity that was successful in expanding the aikido population. The steady accumulation of small things for the last sixty years, I believe, have made our art permeate gradually into society. Let us take a renewed look at the natural course of its history.

Morihei Ueshiba, the Founder of Aikido

Morihei Ueshiba, the Founder of aikido, was born in Nishinotani Village (now Tanabe City), Nishimuro County, Wakayama Prefecture in 1883 (the 16th year of the Meiji era) as a first son of the Ueshibas, a wealthy farming family. The Founder's father, Yoroku, a man with a massive figure and phenomenal strength, was a local magnate who served as member of a village assembly. His mother, Yuki, came from the Itokawa family, based also in Tanabe City.

Morihei Ueshiba,
the Founder of aikido

The Founder was a long-awaited son who was born when Yoroku was forty and, therefore, was bathed in his father's love and affection. He was a delicate, introvert, and bookish infant. He learned the Nine Chinese Classics at a school operated by a local temple on one hand and was absorbed in mathematics and physics experiments on the other. Concerned about the way Morihei spent his days indoors, Yoroku encouraged him to play sumo wrestling with fishermen's children to develop his physical strength. Being by nature a person who hates to lose in anything, he soon grew up to be an active and outgoing boy who enjoyed diving and spearfishing in the sea.

After graduating from Tanabe Secondary School and an abacus school, he got a job at the Tax Office in Tanabe City in 1901 but had to quit the job because of his positive involvement in the 'Beach Incident' (the local fishing folk's conflict for fishing rights and movement against the reformation of the Fisheries Law). In 1902, at the age of nineteen, he resolved to do something new and went to Tokyo to establish Ueshiba Commercial Firm and launch a wholesale business of stationery with his father's help. At the same time he learned jujutsu of the Tenjin-shinyo school and fencing of the Shinkage school. Though successful in his business, he got beriberi and passed the shop to his employee to go back to Tanabe for recuperation. He tried to get over beriberi by running around fields and mountains in bare feet, and this practice proved to be successful and made his body stronger than before.

In 1903 he entered the army at the age of twenty. Around the same time he went to Sakai to become a pupil of Masakatsu Nakai, the master of jujutsu of the Yagyu-shingan school. In the army he proved himself to be outstanding in marching and bayoneting and was regarded as the 'paragon of a soldier' by his colleagues. He even worked as a substitute teacher of bayoneting for his senior officer. Promoted as high as to a sergeant, he was willing to become a professional soldier but dismissed the idea because of his father's objection and went back to Tanabe. In 1908 he got a license of the Yagyu-shingan school from Masanosuke Tsuboi.

After returning to his home, the Founder was spending idle and depressing days, quite at a loss what to do, when Yoroku, unable to leave his son in that condition, converted the barn in his farm into a judo dojo and asked the judo master Kiyoichi Takagi (later promoted to the 9th dan in the Kodokan), who happened to be staying in Tanabe, to teach his art there. The Founder was immediately absorbed in judo, and, with other people from the neighbourhood joining them, the dojo became very lively as if it were an assembly hall for the local youth.

In 1912 (the 45th year of the Meiji era and the first year of the Taisho era) the Founder, in response to the government's policy of inviting cultivating groups to Hokkaido, migrated to Shirataki-genya, Kami-yubetsu Village, Monbetsu County (renamed Shirataki Village and later Engaru Town) at the age of twenty-nine as the leader of the 'Kishu Group' consisting of eighty-odd members from fifty-four families. Those people, born and bred in the mild climate in Kishu, found it extremely difficult to work in the cold untamed fields in Hokkaido but worked very hard not only at logging and clearing but also at constructing a primary school and developing a shopping street and a residential area. As a result, the village got full of life, and he was called the 'King of Shirataki' and revered by villagers.

He also gave shelter to a labourer who had escaped from the residence of a construction site, so wretched as to be called 'prison cells', and had it out with the yakuza gang in charge of the site to rescue him from their rule. When this story spread and reached the ears of other labourers in the similar conditions, quite a number of them escaped from their employers and came to the Founder, asking for help. He saved all of them, and his heroic deed was reported in a local newspaper.

In 1912 he visited a ryokan in Engaru on business, where he met Sokaku Takeda, the martial art master of the Daito school. The Founder was astounded at his martial skills and instantly became his disciple. He further made a dojo in Shirataki and invited Sokaku as its master. Together with ten-odd interested villagers he trained very hard and got a license of his master's 'secret art' in 1915.

In 1918 he was supported by villagers to be elected a member of the Kami-yubetsu village assembly and became a local celebrity of established reputation. The next year, however, he received the news that his father was critically ill and quickly got ready to return home by train. On his way to Wakayama, he heard of the reputation of Onisaburo Deguchi, the substantial leader of the religious sect of Oomoto. The Founder then made

The Founder as member of the Kami-yubetsu village assembly; the second from the left in the front row

a stopover at Ayabe in Kyoto to ask Onisaburo to pray for his father's recovery and was deeply fascinated by his personality. Although his father passed away before his return, he was greatly relieved to hear Onisaburo say 'Everything is all right with your father', and realized that it would be the best service to his late father to calmly accept the way he died a natural death. He went back to Tanabe to perform a funeral service for his father and then, in 1920, migrated to Ayabe with his family to join the faith of Oomoto.

Onisaburo, greatly pleased by his conversion, took him into his service as an attendant and advised him to devote his life to martial arts. The Founder went through a variety of mental training under Onisaburo's tutelage and opened in his house a dojo called 'Ueshiba Juku [School]' on Onisaburo's advice. In Ayabe he supervised training at the dojo as well as group

The Founder in Ayabe 1921

work of young people, based on his experiences in Shirataki, in forming a fire brigade and developing a plantation. In the following year (1921), my father, Kisshomaru Ueshiba, was born, later to be the second Doshu [Leader] of aikido.

During his stay in Tanabe, the Founder got acquainted with Kumagusu Minakata, the great naturalist. He was so impressed with Minakata's movement against shrine consolidation that he joined Minakata together with young followers and local villagers and played an active part in the protest movement. His idea of budo as an art of reconciliation, which should be utilized to make a better and happier world, might have come from his experiences of working with local people as well as from the spirits of 'universal love' and 'harmonious brotherhood' in Oomoto. In 1922 he adopted Onisaburo's suggestion of naming his martial art 'aiki bujutsu' and devoted himself to the study of *kotodama* [the soul of language] and *Kojiki* [Records of Ancient Matters] in the hope of constructing its philosophical basis.

In 1925 the Founder went to Tokyo in response to the invitation of Isamu Takeshita, Admiral of the Japanese Navy, who had heard of his reputation, and demonstrated his skills in front of Gonnohyōe Yamamoto [Count Yamamoto], who, very much impressed, in turn asked him to teach them to his retainers and military officers, which he started accordingly

The Chinese letters indicating 'Ueshiba School' written by Onisaburo

The Founder teaching his pupil at Ueshiba School in
Ayabe circa 1920

at Aoyama Palace. In 1927 (the 2nd year of the Showa era)
he moved to Tokyo and built a temporary dojo at Shiba-
shiroganesaru-machi. In 1928 he moved his dojo to Shiba-
mitatsuna-machi in Shiba through the kindness of Katsujiro
Utsumi [Baron Utsumi]. In 1929 he further moved the dojo
to Shiba-takanawakuruma-cho (by the Sengaku-ji Temple),
where he taught new students. As applicants for discipleship

grew in number, it got more and more difficult to teach them in a temporary dojo, and there were increasing demands that a substantial dojo should be constructed.

In 1930 the Founder rented (later bought) the site in Ushigomewakamatsu-cho (now Wakamatsu-cho in the Shinjuku ward), where the Ogasawaras' villa once stood, and launched the construction of the Kobukan/Ueshiba Dojo (later to be the Aikido Hombu Dojo), which was finished in March the next year. It is worth mentioning in this context that this dojo survived the war and stayed as it was until reconstructed in 1968.

In those days, the dojo was not open to the general public, and those admitted to it were only small classes of people including members of the Imperial family, aristocrats, policemen, businessmen, or martial artists' children. They also had to meet the strict requirements for admission that they should have more than two respectable guarantors and that they should not show their skills publicly. He also gave martial art instruction, at the request of the military authorities, at the Toyama Army School, Military-Police School, Nakano School, and Naval Academy.

Around the same time, he was also requested by Onisaburo Deguchi to teach members of the 'Showa Youth Association', a nationwide unified organization of Oomoto. The consequent rapid expansion of membership led to the establishment of Dainihon Budo Sen'yōkai [the Great Japan Martial Arts Promotion Association], which, with 129 branches and 2488 members, is the Western counterpart of the Kobukan in Tokyo as a base of his art.

Soon Japan plunged into war, and as the war situation took a

The Founder (the third from the left) once gave martial art instruction at the request of the military authorities

sharp turn for the worse, the Founder started to think seriously about how to protect the tradition of aikido and keep it alive. So, in 1935, he bought a land of 3,000 *tsubo* [approximately 9,900 square metres] in Iwama in Ibaraki Prefecture (now the City of Kasama) in prospect of realizing the idea, which he had cherished long since, of 'self-sufficient lifestyle' and 'unification of martial arts and agriculture'. After that he bought more of the neibouring land, and the total area in 1940 amounted to approximately 20,000 *tsubo*. In 1942 he entrusted the dojo in Tokyo to my father, Kisshomaru, who was at that time still an undergraduate student of Waseda University, and started a life of martial arts and agriculture combined, cultivating land in Iwama and teaching aikido to local people. Meanwhile, Kobukai, the predecessor of Aikikai, was authorized by the then Ministry of Health and Welfare to become a juridical foundation.

The Founder (left) and Kisshomaru the second Doshu (right; Director of the Hombu Dojo at the time, who later made aikido accessible to the general public) in front of the Hombu Dojo in the mid 30s of the Showa era

Kisshomaru, the Second Doshu's Hope of 'Making Aikido Accessible to the General Public'

Going back into the history of aikido, we always get to the undeniable existence of a martial art genius called Morihei Ueshiba, from whom everything started. However, this Founder of aikido taught what was then called 'aiki-budo' only to the limited number of people with respectable references including soldiers, aristocrats, and reputable businessmen in fear of its misappropriation. The spread of aikido was made possible rather by other people who understood the true value of the art, such as Isamu Takeshita, Admiral of the Japanese Navy, who invited the Founder to Tokyo, Mr. Kozaburo Okada, who introduced the Founder's budo to businessmen and financiers, Mr. Kin'ya Fujita, who strongly recommended the establishment of a juridical foundation, Mr. Teruzo Miyasaka, who provided funds for establishing a foundation. Here came on the scene Kisshomaru Ueshiba, the second Doshu, who made the basic arrangement of our organization in order to make the Founder's aikido accessible to the general public. It is largely because of his keen insight and untiring devotion to the job that aikido is now practiced on a global scale.

In 1942 'aiki-budo' was renamed 'aikido', and in the same year Kisshomaru the second Doshu (then aged 21) became Director of the Hombu Dojo of the Kobukai Foundation. He was still an undergraduate student at Waseda University. The Founder is reported to have said to him, 'You take care of social activities; I'll spend the rest of my life practicing aikido'. The Pacific War had broken out in the previous year, and everything took on a wartime look.

On August 15th, 1945, the war ended. The Founder's order to 'defend the jodo to the death' was strictly obeyed, and the dojo survived the large-scale air attack right before the end of the war. The dojo provided shelter to local war sufferers, who reportedly amounted to more than a hundred at one time. Some of them stayed there after I was born, and I still remember there lived two families until I was five years old. Even though the dojo survived the wartime fire, it is hard to imagine what the second Doshu felt when he saw the whole stretch of the burned-out ruins of Japan.

Kisshomaru the second Doshu, vacantly listening to the Emperor Showa's announcement of Japan's surrender, fell prostrate upon the gravel ground before the Imperial Palace with one of his friends and shed bitter tears, as he told me later. He had also lost many friends who had been sent to the front as student soldiers. I still remember my father silently bowing every time we drove by Yasukuni Shrine on the way to the Nippon Budokan [Martial Arts Arena]. The feeling of utter mortification and wish for the repose of the dead made him determine to spread his father's art—that is, the art of aikido, which he confidently believed to be presentable even to the victorious nations—in the hope of rebuilding Japanese people's spirit.

In 1947, still in the midst of postwar confusion, he reorganized the Kobukai Foundation into the 'Aikikai Foundation', which was based in Aiki-en in Iwama, and applied to the Ministry of Education for a revision of its articles of association. The Ministry's approval was granted in February the next year, and consequently Morihei Ueshiba became the first Doshu of aikido and Kisshomaru Ueshiba the Director of the Hombu Dojo. From this year on, the latter devoted himself to the promotion of aikido as head of organization. In 1949 he resumed regular training and in 1951 brought the Hombu Dojo from Iwama back to Tokyo.

The basic principle he set up at that time was to 'make aikido accessible to the general public'. Budo is of little value in the modern world unless it can be practiced by anyone regardless of age and is related to our everyday lives in some way or other—

The second Doshu who resumed regular training and further launched a project of 'making aikido accessible to the general public'; photographed circa 1958

this was what he always told us as his ideal of martial arts. This was also the point from where aikido started to expand. The policy of 'making aikido accessible to the general public' penetrates through all our activities of sending instructors to clubs at universities as well as to those in foreign countries, organizing public demonstrations, opening classes at centres for cultural education, publishing books on aikido, and so on and so forth.

From a purely financial point of view, it would definitely be far more paying to teach executive officers rather than normal working adults, working adults rather than students. However, in sharp contrast to the way the Founder admitted only the cream of society into his dojo in the prewar period, the second Doshu took a totally different admission policy and promotion strategies. He found it a better idea to place a solid foundation of aikido on associations of students, many of whom then would continue to practice aikido after going out into the world and distinguishing themselves and in turn make the foundation more solid. Japanese universities of that time, though very limited in number, provided such academic and cultural experiences as to enable their students to exert leadership in society after graduation. He wanted aikido to take root among the coming young generation.

As regards this policy, there were some disagreements. Even a devoted and understanding master of Aikikai reportedly suggested that they should stop sending teachers to those non-profit-making university clubs. Nevertheless, the second Doshu never stopped any of the teaching projects at universities. Although we now understand in retrospect that he made the right choice, he must have experienced a lot of pressure in sticking to the policy without any immediate prospect of success.

Before long those old disciples of the Founder from the prewar period also resumed training and opened many local dojos, which developed themselves into branches (now affiliated dojos) of Aikikai. Furthermore, those trainees from local dojos and university clubs went out into the world and formed aikido clubs of working adults. The idea of promoting aikido in centres of cultural education was first suggested by Mr. Kazuma Nagano, who at that time was one of the committee members of Aikikai, and taken up by the second Doshu, who visited the Sankei Centre of Cultural Education to discuss the possibility of opening aikido classes with the then Executive Director. The idea at first was simply sneered away, but his patient persuasion brought it to fruition. All these efforts brought about the slow but steady promotion of aikido.

The First Public Demonstration

The first public demonstration of aikido was held at the Takashimaya Department Store in Nihon-bashi, Tokyo in September 1955. Before that, nobody in principle was allowed to demonstrate aikido skills except the Founder himself, and opportunities for watching his 'public demonstrations' were strictly limited only to a handful of people. Even in the martial art community, people knew him only by name; only a few of them actually saw him demonstrate techniques.

Secrecy of instruction, I hasten to add, was not a policy peculiar to aikido; other old Japanese martial art schools also kept their skills secret, and when they had to demonstrate some of them in public, only the masters from the respective head families did the job. With the policy of secrecy, the Founder even made a point of keeping all the windows of the dojo closed when he demonstrated his skills so that no one could see them from outside. His cautious attitude towards the promotion of aikido might have come from his apprehension that its possible overpopularity might disrupt proper transmission of his art. Some of the people who actually saw his performance even said, 'Old Ueshiba's skills belong only to this grandmaster. Nobody else will be able to master them. Aikido will die with him.'

If Morihei Ueshiba the Founder were the only person who could master the art and nobody else, it would be impossible to promote aikido in a new age. Kisshomaru the second Doshu thought it necessary to break down old customs and have all the trainees—live-in disciples and normal members alike—appear on the stage to show that everybody would be able to master aikido skills after proper training. The Founder, who had at first disapproved of this idea, finally accepted it after the second Doshu's intense persuasion. 'Aikido is accessible to anyone who goes through proper training.' This is the article of faith the second Doshu really wanted to convey.

At the first public demonstration at the Takashimaya Department Store in Nihon-bashi, Tokyo, posters with aikido pictures were displayed its the show window, and its proceedings were reported by radio and in newspapers. The demonstration went down fairly well with the audience, and *The Throne of Aikido,* a documentary film with the Founder as a hero, was created by the NTV (now the Nippon Television Network Corporation). After this event, promotion campaigns were actively conducted with lecture and demonstration sessions on aikido including those sessions at the Toyoko Department Store in Shibuya, Tokyo (18-20 October, 1957) and the Mitsukoshi Department Store in Ikebukuro, Tokyo (17-18 May, 1958). Thus, the publicity of aikido arose remarkably.

Before these sessions started, an 'aikido demonstration meeting' referred to either of the two sessions, one in spring and the other in autumn, mainly held at the Hombu Dojo for the purpose of demonstrating what aikido students had been practiced. After aikido spread to many parts of Japan, local dojos started to hold their own 'demonstration meetings'. Nevertheless, the Hombu Dojo and other local dojos proved to be too small for bigger demonstration meetings. Then Kisshomaru the second Doshu, thinking 'the time is ripe for the expansion of aikido into society', decided to hold such an annual meeting of 'All Japan Aikido Demonstration' as we know today, where aikido trainees from all over Japan would

The Founder in the midst of performance in the first public demonstration on the rooftop of the Takashimaya Department Store in Nihon-bashi

The posters of the public demonstration displayed on the show window of the Takashimaya Department Store

get together to demonstrate their skills publicly. Thus, in 1960, the first All Japan Aikido Demonstration (then called the first Aikido Demonstration Meeting) was held at the Yamano Hall in Yoyogi, Tokyo, followed by the public demonstration at the Isetan Hall in Shinjuku in 1961 (which was not called 'Aikido Demonstration' because the Founder was in the United States at that time with the invitation by the Hawaii branch

Currently, All Japan Aikido Demonstration is held in May every year at the Nippon Budokan with more than ten thousand participants and spectators from all over the country and abroad.

of the Aikikai Foundation), the second Aikido Demonstration at the Auditorium of the head office of the Asahi Shimbun in Yurakucho in 1962, and the third to sixth Demonstration meetings at the Hibiya Public Hall from 1966 (not held in 65 and 67). The name of 'All Japan Aikido Demonstration' has been used from the fifth meeting. The annual meeting was not held in 1967 because the Hombu Dojo was under construction that year.

In those days there were not so many branches (now affiliated dojos) as there are today, nor did groups of ordinary members perform at those meetings, the programs consisting mainly of masters' demonstrations. One meeting did not last very long, beginning at noon and ending as early as a little after three o'clock in the afternoon.

In 1969 the Founder passed away, and on October 11th

of the same year the meeting of aikido demonstration in his memory was held at the Nippon Budokan [Martial Arts Arena]. It was the first time that we had ever had a meeting of aikido demonstration at the Budokan. Each meeting had had two to three thousand participants previously, but this memorial meeting, as it turned out, attracted five thousand people. The success of this meeting probably brought about the second Doshu's conviction that an annual meeting of aikido demonstration could be a big event suitable to be held at the Nippon Budokan.

After this, the annual meetings up to the 14th in 1976 were held at the Hibiya Public Hall, and in 1977, finally, the venue for the meeting moved to the Nippon Budokan. Participants continued to increase in number, and currently the meeting is the biggest annual event of the Aikikai Public Utility Foundation with more than ten thousand participants and spectators.

Promotion Through Publication

In 1950 the first issue of *The Aikikaiho* [Aikikai Newsletter] (later *The Aikido Shimbun* [Aikido Bulletin]) was published for the purpose of informing aikido students all over Japan of the latest news from local dojos and the Founder's ideas. In 1957 Kisshomaru the second Doshu published *Aikido* from Kowado, which was the first introductory book on aikido published after the war. It so happened at that time that a self-proclaimed martial artist, pretending to open a budo school, swindled the applicants for its membership out of enrollment

The first issue of *The Aikido Shimbun*

Aikido, the first introductory book on aikido published after the war

fees. This fraud case affected the market of budo-related books, and it was extremely difficult to find a bookseller who would be willing to take care of the sales of the book, with the result that its copies were piled high in the dojo. However, its newspaper advertisement brought about a flood of orders, and the first edition sold out.

This book went through several printings till the late 40s of the Showa era, and after its original publisher, Kowado, closed its business, it was reprinted by Shuppan-geijutsu-sha to be a long-time seller, going through many printings again. It made the name of aikido more popular than introductory sessions and public demonstration meetings. The publication of this book seemed to have given the second Doshu the basic framework for clothing aikido in words. His interest in the improvements of methodologies for explaining and teaching the ideals and skills of aikido was also rooted in his strong desire to have this art known to as many people as possible.

After this up to the time he published *Kihan Aikido: Kihon-hen* (The Essence of Aikido: Basics; Shuppan-geijutsu-sha, 1997), which was his last book on aikido techniques, he constantly published many books on aikido in the hope of explaining it in plain language. Many of those books were translated into English, French, Spanish, Italian, and German to be read in many parts of the world, motivating innumerable foreigners to learn aikido. In 1991 the first issue of *Aikido-tankyu* [The Study of Aikido], the official magazine of Aikikai, was published.

Expansion of the Organization

In 1961 university students' associations of aikido were founded one after another as auxiliary organizations of Aikikai, including the Kanto Students' Association of Aikido (founded in June) and the Kansai Students' Association of Aikido (founded in September), to be finally united into the Japan Students' Association of Aikido (founded in October). In December the same year the Ministry of Defense Aikido Association was founded. Furthermore, the Tohoku Students' Association of Aikido, the Kyushu Students' Association of Aikido, the Chubu Students' Association of Aikido, and the Chugoku-Shikoku Students' Association of Aikido were founded respectively in 1963, 66, 67, and 72, and as a result a nationwide aikido-related network of university students was solidly established. Partly because of that, the support of the Ministry of Education was given to the meetings of All Japan Aikido Demonstration since 1967 when the 5th annual meeting was held. The support of a public organization was a clear sign to show that aikido had gained wide social recognition. The seeds that the second Doshu had sowed in spite of financial apprehensions finally bore good fruit.

In 1990 I went to Asia University to give my first aikido lesson at university. In reply to my question whether they knew aikido or not, most of some thirty students there answered that they had heard of it but had no idea what kind of budo it was. Today, in reply to the same question, not a few students mention their experiences of practicing it, reminding me of how it has spread over time. It is a sure sign of the steady progress that local aikido teachers have made with effort. The present prosperity of aikido has strengthened my belief that good things convey themselves naturally.

In December 1968 the ferroconcrete building of the Hombu Dojo of Aikido was completed (of which the inauguration ceremony was held the next year). The Aikido School was opened on its fourth floor and authorized by Tokyo Metropolis as a vocational school. This official authorization suggests that educational effects of aikido were publicly acknowledged. Around the same time, the whole management system of Aikikai was gradually solidified.

On April 26, 1969, as if to have ascertained the passing of one age, the Founder passed away at the age of 86 in his home in the site of the Hombu Dojo. On the same day the government conferred the Third Order of the Sacred Treasure (Senior Grade of the Fifth Court Rank) on him posthumously in honour of his achievements in 'founding and promoting aikido'. He was also presented with the titles of Honorary Citizen of Tanabe City,

Left: the ceremony of purifying the building site of the Hombu Dojo of Aikido

Right: the second Doshu in front of the conceptual drawing of the New Hombu Dojo of Aikido which was to be completed in 1968

Wakayama Prefecture, and Honorary Citizen of Iwama-cho, Ibaraki Prefecture.

In 1976, based on the progress of aikido mentioned above, the Japan Association of Aikido was founded. It was in the same year that the first newsletter of Aikikai was published. At that time the 'list of branch dojos' was printed only across two facing pages, and the number of the dojos was about 120. Today, the number of affiliated dojos ('branch dojos' were renamed as 'affiliated dojos' in 2012) is over 2,400, and we have to print their list and a newsletter in separate booklets. This suggests how the management systems of local dojos have been solidified.

In 2002, the Japan High School Aikido Association was established, and the first meeting of All Japan High School Aikido Demonstration took place in the Tokyo Budokan. In 2012, when budo became a compulsory subject of physical education in the curriculum of junior high school, aikido was adopted as one of the elective martial art subjects. Although aikido was not taken up by many schools, within the same year we already started to organize local aikido leagues all over Japan so that we might be able to meet the needs of instructors who would help as many young people as possible to develop their sound mind and body. It was in the same year that our status changed from a foundation approved by the Ministry of Education to a public utility foundation approved by the Cabinet Office.

Globalization of Aikido: A Silver Bridge

While promoting aikido in Japan, Kisshomaru the second Doshu also endeavoured to promote it in foreign countries so that its values might get worldwide recognition. Promotion of aikido overseas began in 1953 when Master Aritoshi Murashige and his colleagues were invited to the Mandalay Police Academy in Burma (now Myanmar) to teach aikido. While sending instructors abroad, we also admitted international students who came to Japan to study aikido. When André Nocquet came from France in 1955, he drew media attention not only in Japan but also in France as someone who came all the way from a victorious nation in the Second World War to a defeated nation to study one of its martial arts. News reports on such occasions could have been one of the elements that heighten the publicity of aikido.

In 1961 the Founder himself went to Hawaii at the invitation of

Hawaii Aikikai to celebrate the completion of its new dojo, and two years later Kisshomaru the second Doshu went to the United States at the invitation of the American and Hawaii Aikikai Foundations. From around the 40th year of the Showa era onwards, aikido instructors went over to many different parts of the world, mainly

The Founder staying in America at the invitation of Hawaii Aikikai

in Europe and America—Master Hiroshi Tada to Italy, Master Nobuyoshi Tamura to France, Master Yoshimitsu Yamada and Master Mitsunari Kanai to the United States, Master Kazuo Chiba to Britain, Master Seiich Sugano to Australia, Master Katsuaki Asai to Germany, and so on—and stay there for some time to make steady efforts to promote aikido.

In November 1975 the Preparatory Committee for establishing an international federation of aikido was launched in Madrid in Spain. In the committee meeting it was confirmed that the essence of aikido should be sought in the uniqueness of training-oriented Japanese philosophy and that its tradition started with Morihei Ueshiba. It was also confirmed that Doshu, the personified centre of aikido, should be the lifetime president of the federation. In 1976, after the whole process of preparation by the committee, the International Aikido Federation (IAF)

The second Doshu giving a speech at the first
meeting of the IAF

was officially founded to strengthen the international network
of aikido-related organizations. The first general meeting of the
IAF was held in Tokyo with about four hundred participants
from twenty-nine countries including the United States. The
establishment of the IAF and the All Japan Aikido Federation,
which was also founded in the same year, clearly marks the
point where the whole management system of aikido-related
organizations was built up inside and outside Japan.

After the establishment of the IAF the project of sending
instructors abroad got more activated, and on the other
hand, incoming foreign aikido students and participations in
intensive training sessions increased in number, with the result
that aikido-related international exchanges between many
different parts of the world were very much promoted. In 1980
travelling instruction sessions in South-East Asia started. In
1980, at the request of Papua New Guinea, we sent two aikido

instructors as members of the Japan Overseas Cooperation Volunteers (JOCV) for the first time, and after this the project of sending instructors as JOCV members got well under way.

In 1984 the IAF joined the General Association of International Sports Federation (GAISF) as a regular member. The GAISF, the second largest international sports organization after the International Olympic Committee (IOC), aims to put together international organizations of sports and promote the exchange of opinions among them. The IAF is the only international organization in the GAISF that aims at the promotion of aikido.

In 1989 (the 1st year of the Heisei era) aikido was adopted for the first time in its history as one of the public games in the World Games held in Karlsruhe in Germany. In 1990, just as the Soviet Union was disintegrated, trainees from Bulgaria and the Russian Republic, two of the countries in the Communist bloc, came to Japan to undergo training at the Hombu Dojo, which was totally unthinkable in the age of the Cold War. The promotion of aikido in Eastern Europe and Central Asia has been so well under way that we have been requested to send instructors, who go to those parts of the world on a regular basis and now teach one hundred twenty sessions every year. In 1994 the first general meeting of Asian Aikido Demonstration was held in Taipei, followed by many remarkable events and activities in foreign countries, with the result of an increasing number of trainees as I notice myself during my trips to them. I am truly convinced that the popularity of aikido among foreign people is based on their recognition of the universal values of the art as a way of mental and physical training beyond the racial, religious, and national borders.

The training session commemorating the 150th anniversary of Japan-Belgium friendly relations (2016)

Nowadays, so many active projects for promoting aikido in foreign countries are being carried out not only by Aikikai but also by other organizations including the Japan Foundation and the Japan International Cooperation Agency (JICA) which delegate many aikido instructors as participants in exchange programmes, JOCV members, and senior volunteers. At present there are aikido lovers in almost all countries except those in Africa and some parts of Middle East where political situations are extremely instable. In 2004 we were awarded a commendation by the Minister of Foreign Affairs for contributing to the promotion of international cultural exchange and friendship between many nations through aikido.

When the Founder visited America in 1961 at the invitation of Hawaii Aikikai, he said 'Aikido is going to be a silver bridge between Japan and the rest of the world.' His dream and ambition, which were handed down through Kisshomaru the second Doshu to me, finally came true thanks to the efforts of

The author receiving a commendation from the then Minister of Foreign Affairs, Yoriko Kawaguchi, in 2004 for contributing to the promotion of international cultural exchange

The author and his wife, Kyoko, attending the Autumn Garden Party held at the Akasaka Imperial Gardens by Their Majesties in 2004 after receiving a commendation from the Minister of Foreign Affairs

travelling instructors and local aikido lovers.

I feel a slight hesitation in expressing my passionate admiration for Kisshomaru the second Doshu, because he is also my father. Be that as it may, he was a role model for me. He always thought calmly about things, not jumping to a passing whim on the spur of the moment or driven by emotions, took an objective look at them with constructive ideas in mind, solved problems one by one, and made aikido accessible to the general public. I have always tried to follow his example even after his death and devoted myself to the promotion and popularization of aikido.

One manifestation of the successful promotion of aikido was the training session I taught during the 12th General Meeting of Aikido in 2016, in which nearly two thousand members of Aikikai took part. Master Hiroshi Tada, the highest-ranking active master of aikido, who was looking at our training from the balcony of the arena, feelingly said, 'O-sensei [the Founder] would have been very much pleased to see this', as I was told later.

Internationalization of aikido is very much affected by the recent development of communication technology. We used to correspond with people overseas by airmail, spending several weeks in communicating with each other, but we now have electric mail which is a much faster means of international communication. Now that aikido has spread to one hundred and forty countries and regions with a consequent increase of the aikido population, the amount of jobs concerning international communication is growing larger and larger day by day. It is necessary for the Hombu Dojo, I believe, to deal with them as quickly as possible. It is also getting more

The author demonstrating a technique in front of nearly two thousand trainees from inside and outside Japan at the 12th General Meeting of the IAF held at the Takasaki Arena in Takasaki City, Gunma Prefecture in 2016

and more important for us to provide the latest aikido-related information to the world, not only by publishing such bulletins and magazines as *Aikido Newsletter* and *Aikido Tankyu* but also by updating our Website.

In order to cope with these unprecedented situations, which will be extremely difficult for individuals to handle, it is essential for the Aikikai staff and members of local dojos to work in collaboration with each other. I am convinced that it is my duty to convey and spread the Founder's art of aikido properly with the help of all those people.

Training Methods and Spiritual Teachings of Aikido

The Essence of Aikido as a Contemporary Martial Art Is Love

The Founder said 'The essence of budo is love'. It would have been revolutionary in those days when he practiced martial arts, I guess, to characterize martial arts with reference to the concept of 'love'. Years later, Kisshomaru the second Doshu said, 'Aikido is a contemporary martial art'. As the present Doshu, I wish to be a consistent follower of these ideas and hand down aikido to posterity.

After going through the hardships of wartime during the Second World War, the Founder attained a full understanding of what his art should be, which was most appropriately expressed by the proposition 'aikido is love'. Kisshomaru the second Doshu often said, 'Aikido cannot be called a modern martial art unless it has a role to play in the modern world'.

As a way of putting this idea into practice, we are provided with the training methodology unique to aikido. We do not contend for physical superiority but make a point of applying techniques on each other. In practicing them, we are expected to respect our training partners and be nice to each other. As we all have to depend on many other people, it is important to make use of what we mastered through training in society. Of course, being an aikido trainee does not always mean being able to do that, but every trainee has to bear the importance in mind in training.

The author teaching a session in the Hombu Dojo

The Guidlines for Practcing Aikido

In the Hombu Dojo we have 'The Guidelines for Practicing Aikido', which the Founder left us, for all its trainees' reference:

1.   As aikido is so powerful as to let you have your opponent's life in your hand in a single move, you need to follow your teacher's instructions in practicing it and refrain from contending for physical strength in vain.

2.   As aikido is a way of making it possible for one to cope with many opponents single-handed, you need not only to look ahead but also to imagine yourself facing your opponents in all directions.

3.   Practice aikido in such a way that you enjoy it.

4.   Your teacher shows you only a fragment of aikido; you have to make strenuous efforts in training to realize how to use

it to master the whole art.

5.　It is important in your daily training to begin by moving your body lightly and gradually proceed to harder training in such a way that you do not overwork yourself too much. If you practice this method, you can keep on training pleasantly without damaging any part of your body and attain the goal irrespective of your age.

6.　As aikido aims to create citizens of integrity through mental and physical training with secret techniques, you must abstain from showing aikido skills openly to outsiders or letting hoodlums make a bad use of them.

These guidelines are further explicated in *Aikido no Kokoro* [The Spirit of Aikido], written by my father, Kisshomaru the second Doshu, as follows:

1.　Unless you refrain from practicing aikido simply on your own and follow your teacher's instructions, you cannot master aikido properly.

2.　It is extremely important in practicing aikido as a martial art to be constantly on the alert in every direction and stay mentally and physically at your peak.

3.　If you keep on doing hard training until you stop feeling it painful, then you start enjoying training.

4.　You need to abstain from satisfying yourself by learning just the groundwork of aikido at dojo and constantly think about how you can make what you have learned your own.

5.　It is important to practice aikido in such a way that you keep the proper way of training, considering your physical strength, daily physical conditions, and age, in order to keep training for a long time.

6.   The major aim of aikido being to elevate your own humanity, you must strictly refrain from showing off your aikido skills to others.

In the Founder's 'Guidelines for Practicing Aikido', there is a terse but at the same time profound phrase, 'Practice aikido in such a way that you enjoy it'. This is a really important message for us to cherish in practicing aikido. Concerning the third article of the Guidelines, there is a supplementary note by the Founder himself:

> Martial arts tend to be associated with a feeling of tragic heroism with which one stiffens his shoulders and forearms, but it is the image of an immature trainee trying to conceal his lack of skills and confidence and just putting on a bold front. On the contrary, martial artists with proper skills tend to look graceful without any stiffness in their muscles, and those with true confidence tend to look composed and always have an expression of 'pleasantness' on their faces. They are gentle in appearance but tough inside, ordinarily quiet and modest, and natural and unaffected in the way they behave. In short, those who are able to present themselves as they really are and to live their own lives as they like can be called true trainees of martial arts.

Based on the Founder's 'Guidelines' and Kisshomaru the second Doshu's explications in *Aikido no Kokoro*, here I propose to add my own explanations:

1.   As long as aikido is a martial art, its techniques are potentially 'so powerful as to let you have your opponent's life in your hand in a single move'. Forced moves, whether based on your technical inexperience, lack of concentration, or sense of technical or physical competition, may cause injury to your training partners or to yourself. It is important to follow your teacher's instructions in practicing aikido.

2.   Be ready to cope with all sorts of attacks from all directions. In order to make it possible in training, you should not focus just on one object or thing but take a survey of the whole. In so doing, you develop the mental and physical abilities with which you can be attentive to and on guard against everything that is happening around you. Therefore, you need to practice every technique repeatedly until you master the skill of using it properly regardless of your partners or attacking variations.

3.   If I am to add my own words to Kisshomaru the second Doshu's explanation, I would tell you that the 'enjoyment' of training arises when you neither feel unpleasant nor make others feel so. Enjoyment may be associated with smiley faces, but we hardly practice aikido in such a cheerful atmosphere where trainees are always smiling or laughing. Do not do to others what you do not like them to do to you. Fulfilling training is possible when trainees take care not to make others feel unpleasant, take turns in practicing techniques, and elevate each other mentally and physically. It is also a kind of training which will make you feel refreshed afterwards. You will really enjoy keeping on such training every day. It must be fairly pleasant to pursue it on your own without being forced to do anything. In order to understand this, you have only to see

those aikido students who are leaving their respective dojos after their daily training.

4. Aikido teachers demonstrate techniques so that you can master them. Training begins by imitating your teacher's movements, but, as long as you are not the same person as your teacher, it is impossible to do it just the way he or she did. Instead, the important thing is to rightly understand what you learned from your teacher as the very basics to be applied in your own way.

5. The first step is to limber up and warm up by practicing some of the basic bodily movements that constitute the central frameworks of aikido techniques. By maintaining your own way of training according to your physical strength and skills, you can keep on with training irrespective of 'age', as the Founder's fifth Guideline says, as well as of sex, without injuring any part of your body, and inevitably master target techniques.

6. Aikido aims to create citizens of integrity. Citizens of integrity are the people who can communicate sincerely with other people. As I suggested in reference to the first guideline, aikido techniques contain dangerous elements. If you bear the slightest desire to try your newly acquired techniques on other people or show off the efficiency of your skills, not to mention the ill feeling with which you wish to injure people or make them suffer, you cannot be called a true citizen of integrity.

The Ideals of Aikido Lie in Its Training Methodology Itself

The Founder expressed the ideals of aikido with such phrases as 'the martial art of harmony', 'the way of preserving the welfare of all things in nature', and 'the essence of martial arts is love'. In other words, aikido is the way to create citizens of integrity, who also have sincerity and a sense of proportion in communicating with other people.

These ideals of aikido are embodied by its training methodology itself. In aikido, we practice techniques by turns, sometimes applying them as *tori* on our training partner(s) and at other times serving as *uke* to have them applied on ourselves. We also take care of the balance of techniques we practice. In aikido, there are *nage* [throwing] techniques, *nage-katame* [throwing and grappling] techniques, and *katame* [grappling] techniques, each of which has standing, sitting, and half-sitting-half-standing (with *tori* sitting and *uke* standing) variations. They also have right/left, *omote* [front]/*ura* [back] variations, which we respectively practice the same number of times. We keep on practicing techniques until we overcome our weak points and master all of their variations in a well-balanced way.

In aikido, we do not vie for superiority, physical strength, or victory. Aikido aims to help learners take a good look at their training partners, in practicing the same techniques in turns, understand the partners, and elevate each other mentally and physically. In so doing they cultivate the spirit of harmony, with which they accept and respect each other.

In order to master techniques you need to make sure of the

accuracy of practice. You need to take care that you do not vie with your partners for physical strength and that *tori* should not use any throwing or holding techniques in a tormenting way. *Uke* should also take break-falls naturally and refrain from trying too hard to make technique ineffective. If you do what you should do properly and naturally, your partners will surely realize how they should respond. In order to ensure the accuracy of training, it is also important to take mutual consideration of your partner's skills, physical features, physical strength, or character, and improve each other's skills based on the consideration. This is not to encourage you, of course, to be collusive in training; when you are to strike, you need to strike properly, and when you are to grapple, grapple properly. It is important to use techniques naturally and properly.

We are all emotional beings, of course. Therefore, you may be sometimes influenced by a sense of superiority or antipathy, especially when you are a novice trainee, depending on your partners. It is important, however, to learn to control those feelings through training. In order really to respect others, you need to have the strength to face and control your negative feelings. You should not forget that you need your training partners to practice aikido.

It is not very difficult to understand those feelings with which you try to compete with other people or improve your skills. However, if your training is too much influenced by them, it will not longer be the training of aikido. Techniques do not work well when they feel unpleasant or uncomfortable to your partners. A slightest intention of tormenting others will present itself as the stiffness of your body, which then makes your partners stiffen in anticipation of painful movements. You can practice no accurate techniques under such conditions. You should not do what you do not want other people to do to you. If you do to others what you do not want to be done to yourself, it will surely make them unpleasant. Unpleasant acts quite often generate vengeful feelings and further create a discordant atmosphere among trainees.

This may also be the case with our society in general. I make a point of avoiding negative expressions in communicating with other people. Negation prevents us from going forward. Instead, first I listen to people, and then, even if some disagreement arises, I try to think calmly about it. I observe them carefully and try to find out the best solution between us without imposing my opinion on them or accepting everything they say. The most desirable thing for us is that all aikido students learn through training how to communicate with people and how to keep a proper distance with them and then make use of those skills in their daily lives.

The Founder said, 'When you move, a technique presents itself'. A technique is not something you force on your opponent in confrontation with him or her. You cannot unbalance others simply by pushing or pulling them forcefully; instead you move and bring them naturally into an off-balance position. One of the goals of aikido training is to acquire the sense of techniques working naturally with reasonable bodily movements.

There are so many different aikido students in terms of gender, age, height, weight, length of arms and legs, flexibility, muscular strength, skills, character, and social experiences. You need to carefully observe and understand your training partners so that you can practice techniques with any type of trainees. Repeated training experiences will improve your ability to respond properly to others. Through training you will also learn to take a broad view of things, keep a proper distance with people in consideration of their feelings, respect and understand them, and further acquire an integrated personality.

One of the important things to remember concerning aikido training is to take care that it should not be a one-way experience. Even though you are physically stronger and more experienced than your partners, you need to respect them, once you are in dojo, and work with them on equal terms. You have to refrain from stopping their movements at every turn of training to explain what they should or should not do or showing off your skills; instead you need to hold them in respect. What is important is to take a renewed look at your own physical condition, attitude, ways of thinking, and mind while working with your partners and improve yourself. This is not possible when you are self-centred. I believe that one knows and improves oneself only in relation to other people.

The Importance of Keeping an Open Mind

At training sessions, teachers first demonstrate and explain techniques, and then their students practice them with some different partners. They normally do not teach every student one by one. In referring to a type of budo training we use an expression '*mitori-geiko*' [observation training]. Students carefully observe their teacher's movements, stances, techniques of timing, etc., and then imitate and practice what they have observed until they experience it physically and make it their own. This is a learning strategy of 'stealing your master's techniques with your eyes', which used to be prevalent not only in budo but also in many other traditional fields of artists, craftsmen, and businessmen. I was born into a budo family, grew up in close contact with aikido, and naturally learned its techniques untaught, just by seeing them practiced at dojo. There used to be novice students with some experiences of other martial arts or sports, and they accepted such a training and learning style fairly naturally.

However, as time went by, the number and variety of aikido beginners widened in terms of age or aim for training—with a certain percentage of students practicing aikido for maintaining physical fitness or developing physical strength, for example— and we found it difficult to stay with the traditional way of training. As our society and surroundings change, we need a more systematic methodology for training which can meet the demand of any level of learners. The beginners who have just entered dojo need to have their instructions explained carefully in words.

We used to have beginners in normal classes because we had no policy of streaming. What we did was gather them first to give them some elementary instructions during normal classes and then to encourage them to join others to practice techniques. The basic assumption was that it was the quickest way to master techniques, but now we have a new policy of teaching beginners separately in beginner's classes for the first couple of month after their entrance to dojo. It is partly because a considerable number of aikido students, especially in recent years, seemingly prefer to have verbal instructions—'this

The author at work during a special training session at the Ibaraki Branch Dojo with the participants watching his demonstration; when you are taking a lesson, it is important to 'keep an open mind' in 'observing your teacher's every movement'.

is the reason why we move the arm this way at this time', 'the reason why we practice this movement repeatedly is that it is useful in this technique', and so on—before actually practicing techniques or get a real feeling of being taught when instructed verbally.

Some people try to study and understand in detail the theories on the structure and mechanism of the human body or the movements of muscles. However, aikido techniques themselves are based on the study of those things, and therefore I want them to learn the techniques physically before thinking about them theoretically. The more concerned you are about theories, the less flexible you tend to be in training. Kisshomaru the second Doshu said, 'We are practicing budo and not "studying" about it. There is a world of difference between the two.' It is strange that the tendency to 'study' aikido can be more often seen in students advanced in age than younger ones.

The old tradition of observe-and-learn style of training seems to be more acceptable to elementary-school and junior-high-school students and young people. They do not need detailed explanations but just move around together with us and naturally learn techniques physically. 'The younger, the quicker' is a phenomenon normally observed in relation to learning in general; it is also the case the other way round: the older, the slower. This is not necessarily the matter of physical skills or athletic capacities but comes from young people's 'straightforwardness' that enables them to keep an open mind to anything without being hindered by knowledge or experience. They are much closer to babies who are born, simply observe what their parents, brothers and sisters, and other members of their family do, and naturally absorb what they have observed.

As we grow old, we get to have many things absorbed into our mind and body. When we try to do something new, we may unwittingly allow them to hinder our new attempts, even though we believe ourselves to be keeping an open mind. When you learn something, you need to make your mind a tabula rasa and simply accept your teacher's instructions and model performances. Put aside your questions, and then observe and accept what you are shown. Only when that does not work well, then ask yourself, 'What's wrong?' If you are too concerned with questions and explanations, training does not go well. Do not rely too much on your intellect, but just observe and simply imitate what your teacher shows you, and that way you

The author at work during a special training session in Argentina in 2017 with the participants trying to take in his every instruction; we can see how the tradition of 'stealing your master's techniques with your eyes' has been globalized.

can practice more techniques and naturally improve your skills more quickly.

True, every movement has its own technical points to be remembered concerning how to use your knife hand [*shuto*], how to grapple and grab, how to move your feet, when to make a move, and so on. It is not easy, however, to remember them all from the beginning and master them instantly. You need to grasp a technique and its process not fragmentally but as an organic whole. It consists of its own proper positioning, ways of using *irimi* and *tenkan* movements and unbalancing your opponent, those of utilizing a *kokyu* power and bring them into

After the teacher demonstrates a technique, the students practice it on each other; the teacher also joins them, walking around the dojo.

a certain position to throw or grapple them. You just repeat it over and over again and gradually see its important points. Then, you take a careful look at how your teacher demonstrates it again, make use of your observation in your own training, and make it your own.

When you try to create a work of painting, you first map out a general plan on the canvas and then proceed to paint the details. Aikido training also goes through the same process: you observe a model carefully, shift your mental focus from the whole of a technique to its details, as if to draw and paint them, and complete your own technique. Instructors, therefore, need to improve their own skills every day so that they may demonstrate techniques of high quality and at the same time faithful to the basics of aikido. Students, on their part, need to take a positive attitude towards their lessons; instead of just waiting to 'be taught', they should try to 'absorb' and 'acquire' what they have learned. Instructors are expected not so much to 'teach' as to 'show' good models and 'guide' students. Each daily training session is a good opportunity to make you a tabula rasa. There you refresh yourself and get back to your daily life. This is a precious experience that is hardly attainable in our everyday lives and will surely make all the trainees' lives richer.

Posture and Stance

When you practice a technique with your training partner, you should not pull yourself up a fighting posture; what you need to do is to take a natural posture and stance so that you can move around smoothly. Technically speaking, you stand diagonally towards your partner, keep balance in the lower half of your body with the centre of gravity in your lower abdomen, and take a relaxed posture so that you can move smoothly to the front, back, right, or left to cope with any possible situation. Take a broad view of your opponent, not just one part of his or her body, so that you can respond to any attack or movement in time. Put the other way round, if you take a proper stance, you can inevitably observe the whole of your opponent. If you are too close to your opponent, you cannot see the whole of your opponent's body; if too far, you cannot feel his or her subtle movements or signs of movements. You need to keep your opponent at a proper distance, not too long and not too short.

Take a different stance according to your opponent's physical

Take a natural posture and keep your opponent at a proper distance so that you can take a broad view at his or her whole.

constitution. If you are practicing a technique on a bigger person than you, you stand a little farther away from him or her. If you are too close to the bodily centre of a big opponent, you tend to be tugged into the sphere of his or her power and therefore cannot move smoothly. On the contrary, when you face a smaller person than you, you stand closer to him or her; otherwise, you may tug your opponent into the centre of your body, and your technique will not work well.

This is what we call the basics. However, depending on your opponent's explosive power or technical skills, minor differences always arise. It is not wise to have a fixed idea about your training partners. Try not to have preconceived ideas but to be able to cope with any situation. It is important, in any field or discipline I think, to carefully observe and at the same time get rid of your prejudices and preconceptions; to make yourself a clean slate and keep a flexible attitude towards things without any preconceived ideas about people. In order to make it possible in aikido, it is necessary to practice techniques with a variety of people in a well-balanced way and thereby to learn how to keep a proper stance and develop your martial sensitivity and composure.

Let me repeat once again the importance of taking a broad view. If you are too concerned with small bits and pieces of human relationship, you will be strongly influenced or preoccupied by your own preconceived ideas about people. A broad and comprehensive view of things and people is the key to the attainment of the posture that will enable you to cope with any situation. If you find someone disagreeable, take a comprehensive look at the person with an open mind, and you will surely discover his or her good or attractive points. Then, your preconceived ideas about the person will vanish. By keeping up with your training, you will naturally acquire such an attitude towards people.

Basic Body Movements—*Irimi, Tenkan, Tenshin*, and *Tenkai*

Four of the body movements, which constitute the basic framework of aikido techniques, are *irimi, tenkan, tenshin,* and *Tenkai*. Using these movements in combination, you unbalance, throw, grapple, and pin them.

Irimi is a movement in which you avoid colliding with your opponent's force and dodge an attack, sliding quickly in a single line into his or her side or dead angle. You can also use this movement to move towards the centre of your opponent's body and break his or her central line of attack. *Tenkan* is a movement in which you use the turning force or rotatory power of your body, deal with your opponent's attack in a circular motion and throw him or her off balance. You take an oblique stance, put your front leg a step farther, slide into your opponent's dead angle, and bring him or her into the centre of your rotation. *Tenshin* is a movement in which you first move sideways and, turning around, dodge the attack. The instant your opponent moves to attack you, you bring your back foot farther back and, with your weight on the foot, sweep your front foot behind you. You use the force of attack and unbalance your opponent in a circular motion. *Tenkai* is a movement in which you take an oblique stance and make a 180-degree turnabout on both of your feet.

These four movements are used characteristically in aikido to avoid colliding with your opponent's force and unbalance him or her in a circular motion. The whole set of these movements is described as the 'Law of Circular Motion'. Proper application of this rule is only possible when your body axis is stable. In order to keep the centre of your body stable, you need to practice basic body movements over and over again. Using the movements properly and thereby maximizing the efficiency of motion and force of your body, you throw your opponent off balance and apply techniques on him or her.

Kokyu-Ryoku and *Kokyu-Ho*

The word '*kokyu-ryoku*' refers to the power that is effectively exerted through natural and structurally reasonable movements of your body. The word '*kokyu*' (which literally means 'breathing') should not be misunderstood as referring simply to the act of taking air into your lung and expelling it or as a metaphor for fixing the right timing.

In order to explain how '*kyoku-ryoku*' works, here I take for an example the act of drinking tea. When you drink tea from a teacup you hold, you do not stiffen your shoulders or forearms. You bring the teacup closer to you and then to your mouth smoothly. Another good example is a move we make when we lift up something on the floor. What we do normally is to bend our knees and squat down. In either case, we do not use any extra force but unconsciously make structurally natural movements, which at the same time are the most effective. In the same way, *kokyu-ryoku* is effectively exerted out of your natural posture, which is free from any extra force. The training method for developing *kokyu-ryoku* is called '*kokyu-ho*' [literally 'breathing method']. You learn how to transmit the whole force of you body from its centre through your hands to your partner who is holding them. This is a method we never fail to practice at the end of each training session.

In order to make a proper use of body movements and *kokyu-ho* in a flow of techniques, you need not only technical and bodily training but also concentration and composure that you acquire only after experiencing a lot of training. You also need to adjust yourself to your partner's feelings, physical construction, movements, and speed. You should not allow yourself to be affected by your own desire to look good or subjugate your opponent. Such a desire will not only convey itself to training partners, putting them on alert, but also stiffen you and prevent you from moving naturally. You should try not to compete but harmonize with your opponent.

In my interpretation, '*ki*' is something that is exerted when your mind and body movements are harmoniously put into one. It is easy to explain these things in words, but it will take a lot of training to become able to practice any technique with anyone. Let me hasten to add in this context that *kokyu-ryoku* is not a special force which can move a heavy thing of hundreds of kilograms or a supernatural power which enables us to blow your opponents away without touching them. It is true that sometimes we see, for example at demonstration sessions, uke standing immobilized, unable to attack a fully alert high-ranking master or jumping of his or her accord in anticipation of a counterattack, and such phenomena are not theoretically impossible. However, they occur only as expressions of martial skills based on the performers' relationships and do not represent any essentials of aikido we aim to learn through everyday training.

It sometimes happens that, even when your power is fully exerted through *kokyu-ho,* you cannot apply techniques properly on your training partner owing to the differences of experience, physical construction or strength. In such cases, however, you do not have to feel 'defeated' or 'frustrated'. In practicing aikido, we do not compete with each other. What we do is to respect your training partners and keep practicing aikido with them to improve your skills. Otherwise it is not

At the end of each session we practice kokyu-ho to develop *kokyu-ryoku.*

aikido training.

The correct posture and steady body axis in making *irimi, tenkan, tenshin,* and *tenkai* movements are important in practicing techniques. In a characteristic flow of aikido techniques we first make a move to avoid the line of attack, unbalance your opponent, making it difficult for him or her to fully exert strength, make the best use of *kyokyu-ho* and maximize your own power in applying techniques. When we apply armlocks or wristlocks in nage, nage-katame, and katame techniques, we take care that the joint should bend in structurally natural directions. We avoid colliding with our opponent's force and bend and lock the joint in such a direction where his or her power is minimized.

It is also characteristic of aikido that you use locking, throwing, and grappling techniques in such a direction where your opponent's power is minimized.

Omote [Front] and *Ura* [Back] Techniques

Each aikido technique can be divided into two subtypes: *omote* [front] and *ura* [back] techniques. Strictly speaking, there are some techniques which only have omote movements. Be that as it may, an *omote* technique can be roughly explained as a technique with which you make an *irimi* movement and move straight into the centre of your opponent's body to unbalance him or her, and *ura* technique as one with which you slide into your opponent's rear side and make a *tenkan* movement to unbalance him or her. If you once make an irimi movement, trying to apply an *omote* technique, but get stuck in collision with your opponent's force, then you may move to his or her rear [*ura*] side, make a *tenkan* movement, and apply another technique. You have to practice techniques till you master both their *omote* and *ura* variations in a well-balanced way. However, it is not a good idea to make a clear and fixed distinction between these two variations. Respond to the ever-changing situation in a more flexible way, using one variation or the other according to your opponent's position, and you will be able to master them more quickly.

From the next page on, I explain, with the help of sequence photographs, basic movements and *kokyu-ho*, the way they are utilized in techniques, and their *omote* and *ura* variations. These are exactly the same as what I try to show at special training sessions and on many other occasions, and it is extremely important for you to understand them in order to master aikido techniques.

Irimi

This is a movement you make to avoid the line of attack, sidestep to your opponent's rear side or dead angle, and take control over him/her.

❶ *Tori* stands face to face with *uke*.
❷ - ❺ The instant *uke* raises his/her knife hand overhead to deliver a blow, *tori* brings his/her back foot extensively into *uke*'s rear side in an *irimi* movement and takes control over his/her neck and hand.

*In aikido, one of the training pair applies a technique on the other. The former is called *tori* and the latter *uke*.

Tenkan

This is a movement you make to step into your opponent's rear side and take control over him/her, utilizing the force of rotation and gravity of your body axis.

❶ *Tori* stands face to face with *uke*.

❷ - ❸ When *uke* grabs tori's wrist, *tori* bring his/her front foot farther into *uke*'s rear side.

❹ *Tori* pivots on the foot and takes control over *uke* with his/her knife hands raised upwards.

Tenshin

This is a movement you make to step aside and steer your opponent's attack in rotating yourself. The instant your opponent aims an attack at you, you bring your back foot farther back and pivot on it, sweeping your front foot behind you. You take advantage of the attack and unbalance your opponent in a circular motion.

❶ *Tori* stands face to face with *uke*.
❷ - ❹ The instant *uke* raises his/her knife hand overhead to deliver a blow, *tori* brings his/her back foot sideways, pivots on the foot, and brings *uke*'s knife hand with him/her, striking at *uke*'s face.
❺ - ❻ *Tori* steps aside and brings *uke* with him in a circular motion.

Tenkai

This is a movement in which you take an oblique stance and make an about-face on both your feet.

❶ *Tori* stands face to face with *uke*.

❷ - ❸ The instant uke grabs *tori*'s wrist, *tori* brings his/her hand sideways, delivering a (fake) blow with the other knife hand, and brings his/her front foot into *uke*'s rear side.

❹ - ❺ *Tori* brings his/her back foot extensively into the same side, swinging his/her knife hand upward, and make an about-face on both his/her feet.

Shomen-uchi Irimi-nage

This is one of the most representative aikido techniques.

❶ *Tori* stands face to face with *uke*.

❷ - ❸ The instant *uke* raises his/her knife hand to deliver a blow, *tori* brings his/her back foot extensively into *uke*'s rear side in an *irimi* movement and takes control over *uke*'s neck and knife hand.

❹ *Tori* unbalances *uke* in a tenkan movement.

❺ - ❻ *Tori* brings *uke* to the tip of his/her shoulder and swings his/her arm upward.

❼ - ❽ *Tori* brings his/her back foot extensively forward and throws *uke* down, swinging his/her arm.

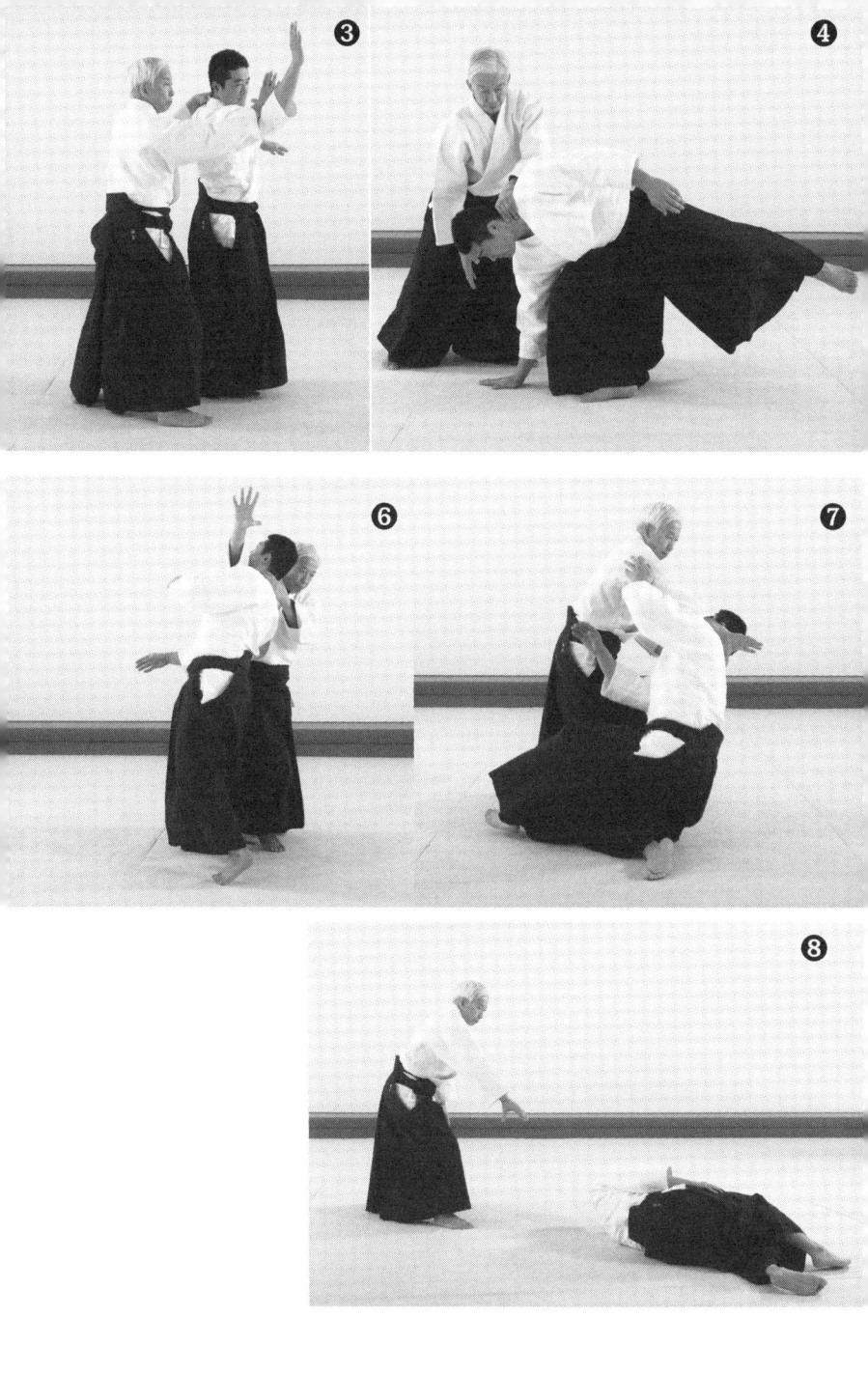

Yokomen-uchi Shiho-nage

This is a technique where a *tenshin* movement plays an important role.

❶ *Tori* stands face to face with *uke*.

❷ - ❸ The instant *uke* raises his/her knife hand to deliver a blow, *tori* brings his/her back foot farther back and steers *uke* in a circular motion, bringing *uke*'s arm down.

❹ - ❺ *Tori* grabs *uke*'s wrist with one hand, puts the other hand on the same wrist and swings both arms upward,

❻ *Tori* turns around and holds *uke*'s wrist.

❼ - ❾ *Tori* swings his/her arms down and brings *uke* down to the mat.

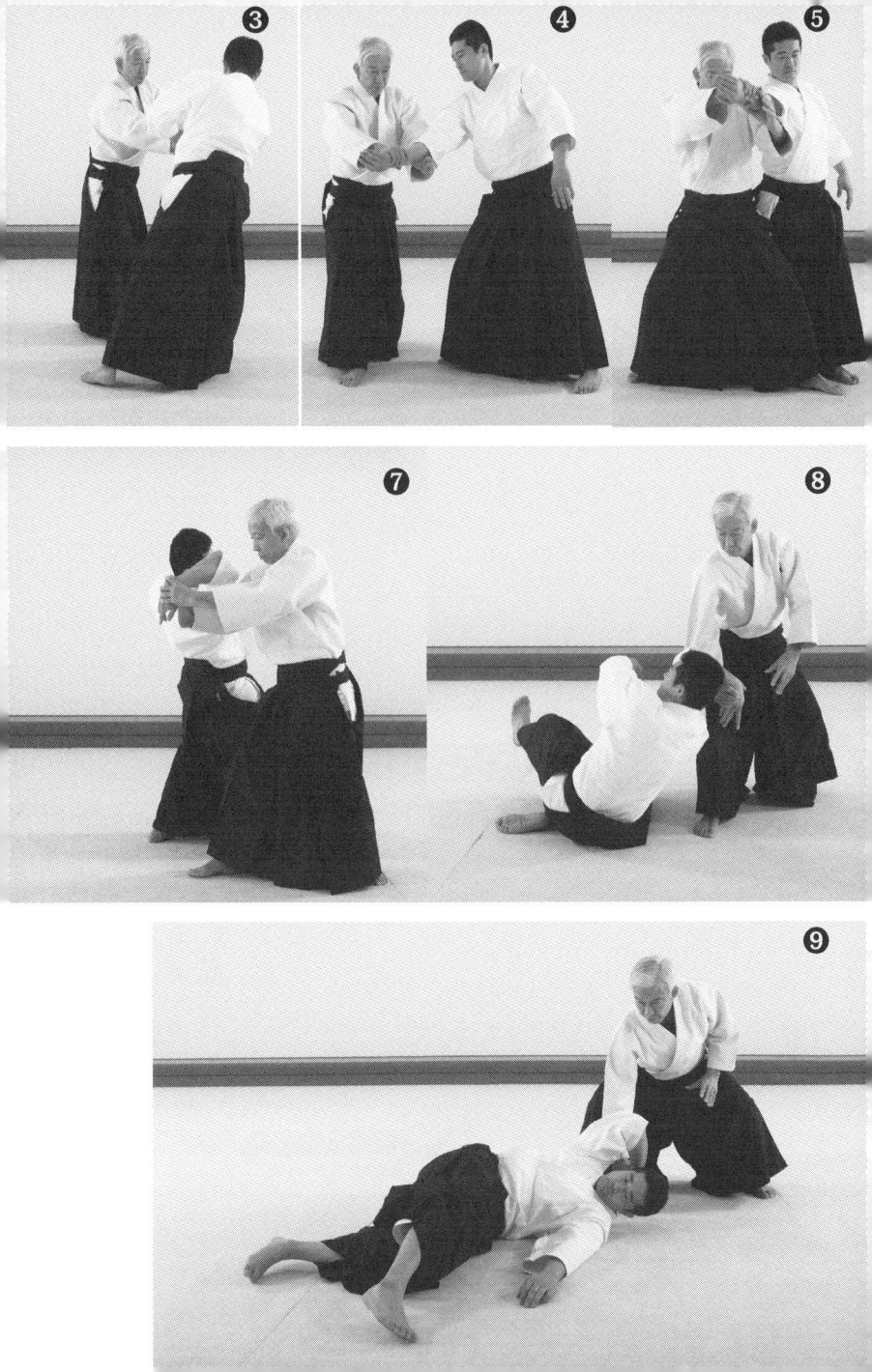

Katate-dori Kaiten-nage

This is a throwing technique where a *tenkai* movement plays an important role.

❶ *Tori* stands face to face with *uke*.

❷ - ❸ The instant *uke* grabs *tori*'s wrist, *tori* swings his/her arm sideways, delivering a (fake) blow at *uke*'s face and brings his/her front leg farther into *uke*'s rear side.

❹ - ❻ *Tori* brings his/her back foot extensively forward, swinging his/her arm upward, and pivot on both foot.

❼ - ❿ *Tori* swings down *uke*'s arm together with his/hers, hold the back of *uke*'s heard and neck, and throws *uke* down to the mat, thrusting his/her arm.

Shomen-uchi Dai-ikkyo (Front)

Here I explain the difference between the front and back techniques, using *dai-ikkyo*, one of the representative grappling techniques in aikido, as an example.

❶ *Tori* stands face to face with *uke*.

❷ The instant *uke* raises his/her knife hand to deliver a blow, *tori* brings his/her front foot diagonally forward, taking control over *uke*'s wrist and elbow.

❸ - ❹ *Tori* steps forward, swinging down *uke*'s arm, and unbalance him/her.

❺ - ❻ *Tori* steps farther forward and brings down *uke* onto the mat with his/her face down, holding down his/her wrist and elbow.

* **❷** - **❹**

In an *omote* [front] variation, *tori* moves straight towards the centre of *uke*'s body in an *irimi* movement.

Shomen-uchi Dai-ikkyo (Back)

❶ *Tori* stands face to face with *uke*.

❷ - ❸ The instant *uke* raises his/her knife hand to deliver a blow, *tori* brings his/her back foot into *uke*'s rear side in an *irimi* movement, taking control over *uke*'s wrist and elbow.

❹ - ❺ *Tori* rotates on the foot he/she took forward in an *irimi* movement, swinging down *uke*'s arm.

❻ - ❼ *Tori* brings down *uke* onto the mat with his/her face down, holding down his/her wrist and elbow.

* ❷ - ❺

 In an *ura* [back] variation, *tori* steps into *uke*'s rear side in an *irimi* movement and unbalance him/her in an *tenkan* movement.

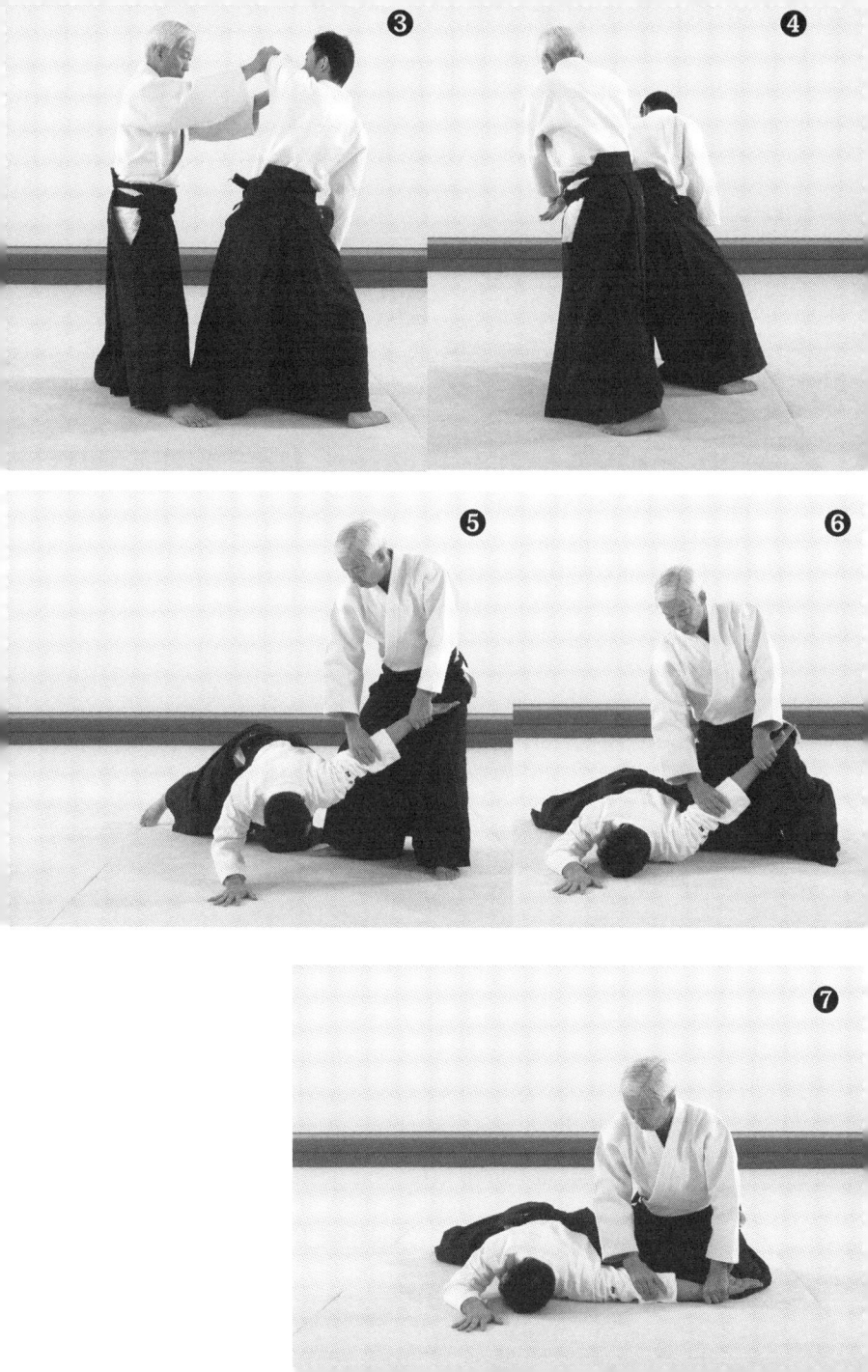

Katate-dori Shiho-nage (Front)

This time I explain the difference between the front and back techniques, using *shiho-nage* as an example.

❶ *Tori* stands face to face with *uke*.

❷ - ❹ As *uke* grabs *tori*'s wrist, *tori* raises his/her knife hand and brings his/her back foot forward, putting the other hand on *uke*'s wrist.

❺ - ❻ *Tori* takes another step forward, swinging his/her arm upward, and makes an about-face, holding *uke*'s wrist.

❼ - ❽ *Tori* brings *uke* down to the mat.

* ❷ - ❻ *Tori* steps forward, swinging his/her arms upward, and unbalance *uke*.

Katate-dori Shiho-nage (Back)

❶ *Tori* stands face to face with *uke*.

❷ - ❹ As *uke* grabs tori's wrist, *tori* steps into *uke*'s rear side in an *irimi* movement and raises his/her knife hand, rotating in a *tenkan* movement.

❺ *Tori* makes an about-face, holding *uke*'s wrist.

❻ - ❼ *Tori* brings *uke* down to the mat.

* ❷ - ❹

Tori steps into *uke*'s rear side in an *irimi* movement, raises his/her knife hand, rotating in a *tenkan* movement, and unbalance *uke*.

Kokyu-ho
(Sitting Position)

Kokyu-ryoku refers to the power you exert from your whole body when you sit in a proper posture and your body functions properly.

❶ *Tori* sits face to with *uke*.
❷ *Tori* lets *uke* grab both his/her wrists with both hands.
❸ *Tori* swings both hands upward.
❹ *Tori* moves one of his/her knees in the direction where he/she tries to bring uke into an off-balance position.
❺ *Tori* takes control over *uke* with his/her face up and pins him/her down with both hands.

* ❸ When you swing your hands upward, take care that your elbows do not move outside, bring your knife hands from below in a circular motion, and try to transmit the force of your whole body through both knife hands.

* ❺ When you pin *uke* down, you put your inside knee against his/her flank and the other knee under his/her wrist.

Morote-dori Kokyu-ho (Front)

❶ *Tori* stands face to face with *uke*.

❷ - ❸ As *uke* grabs *tori*'s wrist, *tori* brings his/her back foot forward and brings his/her knife hand up.

❹ - ❻ *Tori* brings his/her back foot a step deeper into *uke*'s rear side and turn his/her waist, bringing *uke* down onto the mat with both knife hands.

*You step forward in an *irimi* movement and bring your knife hand from the centre of your body upward.

Morote-dori Kokyu-ho (Back)

❶ *Tori* stands face to face with *uke*.

❷ - **❸** As *uke* grabs *tori*'s wrist, tori steps into uke's rear side and brings his/her knife hand up.

❺ - **❻** *Tori* brings his/her front feet to *uke*'s rear side and turn his/her waist, bringing *uke* down onto the mat with both knife hands.

* **❷** - **❹** You step into *uke*'s rear side in an *irimi* movement and bring your knife hand from the centre of your body upward.

Oneness with Heaven and Earth and Agreement with the Law of Nature

The Founder explained the ideal mindset in applying aikido techniques with such phrases as 'oneness with Heaven and Earth', 'placing oneself at the centre of the universe', and 'I am the universe itself'. Those words such as 'universe' and 'heaven and earth' may sound too grandiose to evoke any concrete images, but I think he simply tried to summarize with those words the basics of aikido, which I have explained so far in this book.

You exert your power naturally and effectively in applying techniques, adjusting yourself to your partner's movement, physical constitution and condition. Getting rid of desires for vying for physical strength or for looking good in practicing techniques, you harmonize and blend with your partner by moving in perfect agreement with nature and reason, that is to say, according to the law of physics. Here you reach the point where there is no division between you and the other, where everything is blended into one beautiful entity. It is also the point where there is no feeling of competition, where the ideal of martial arts as love is realized. As you keep practicing aikido, you become able to use techniques spontaneously depending on the situation without trying consciously to do so. Then, at the higher stage, you become one with your opponent with no need of fighting.

Physical Improvement Through Practice

It is often said that aikido needs no power or muscular strength, but what this observation really means is that in aikido you do not use any special power or muscular strength to such an extent that it may prevent your body from functioning smoothly. As you keep practicing techniques and training with other people, you will naturally gain some muscle at the back, even if you are very slim, and find your wrist getting thicker, though, to be sure, no one gets highly muscular only through aikido training. As you practice break-falls repeatedly, you will find your neck stronger and gain more abdominal muscle. Through technical training you will be physically improved. Your body will naturally get strong, and you will gain muscular power that is necessary for applying techniques. Therefore, even when you pair up with a stranger, the very first feel of grip will sometimes tell you how experienced your training partner is.

Since, of course, you need the minimum physical strength for keeping up with training, beginners with no experience in sports are sometimes guided, before they start practicing techniques, to do some supplementary physical exercises in order to become able to take break-falls properly. In university aikido clubs also, new members are instructed to do some supplementary exercises for developing enough physical strength for keeping up with training. However, you do not have to do any special muscle building. The muscle strength needed for aikido can be acquired through aikido training.

It is quite natural, to be sure, that you want to be stronger or seek to do more than ordinary training. We human beings sometimes tend to be overambitious, and I do not necessarily disapprove of all those impatient trial-and-error attempts at elevating oneself. As we grow old and lose muscular strength, we may feel inclined to do something to make up for the loss. However, after long years of training, the loss of muscular strength will be more than offset by the accuracy of techniques, ability to harmonize with training partners, and skills in keeping a proper distance. Otherwise, you cannot be an aikidoist. It is important to remember that muscular strength is not the only one thing needed to practice techniques.

An Overall Ability Displayed as a Result of Consistent and Arduous Training

A point I frequently make at training sessions is that you do not pull but steer your partner to the centre of your body. Aikido techniques are so constructed that you do not 'push' or 'pull' your opponent forcefully but move yourself to 'steer' your opponent into such a position where he/she is naturally unbalanced. If you pull your opponent, he/she reacts in the same way, and there happens a strength contest. The proper image is that, when your opponent grabs your hand or you grab his/her hand, you do not squeeze or tighten your hand but try to exert and transmit the power of your whole body through your arm and hand.

Your mental state directly affects the quality of your movement. This psychosomatic reaction conveys itself to your opponent at the very first contact in training. If you are too much concerned with your opponent or technical manipulations, a competitive atmosphere arises without your knowing it. Then, you stiffen and cannot move in a smooth flow of techniques. This is something very difficult to understand logically. You need simply to feel it.

Some forty years ago, when I graduated from university and started my profession as aikido instructor, I asked Mr. Tadashi Watanabe (former Supervisor of the Aikikai Foundation) to be my training partner. He had long practiced aikido and was of the same generation with my father, so he was far older than I, in his mid-fifties at the time probably. Although I excelled him in physical strength and explosiveness, his movements created an inexpressible atmosphere of maturity and stability. Without any special strength, he used his *kokyu-ryoku* effectively in unbalancing his partner and applying techniques. Then I noted in him the strength that came from his long experience of training, the strength that was totally different from muscular power or youthfulness. This kind of strength may come not only from a trainee's experiences at dojo but also from his or her life philosophy and social experiences. It is what aikido should aim to develop in every student.

Techniques full of strength, explosiveness, flexibility, youthfulness, and vigour are good as they are. It is also pleasant to learn new things in training. You will be advised to absorb in the pleasure at the time. As you keep practicing aikido and grow old, however, you will be more skilled in techniques and maturer as a person and consequently acquire something superior.

'*Do* [the Way]' goes side by side with human life. It is always with you unless you stop pursuing it. Aikido training is part of your life, and you live with it. You concentrate seriously on training, develop your skills, and keep on training with firm belief in aikido. Aikido is a human activity where your life and experience naturally present themselves.

The Essence Lies in the Basics

My father, Kisshomaru the second Doshu, often told me to 'relax your knees, slightly lower your waist, keep your centre steady, and move extensively'. If you strain yourself, your movements will be stiff and limited. On the other hand, if you are too relaxed, you cannot apply techniques very well. His advice possibly was intended to make me properly relaxed without being too conscious of the state.

He also told me that 'minor details of techniques can be mastered through daily training'. Every technique has its own points to mind, but if you are too concerned with their details, you cannot move smoothly. Then you tend to generate friction with your partner and cannot apply techniques properly. The only sure-fire way to improve your skills is to keep on practicing aikido with special focus on its basics and try to grasp with your body the overall movements of techniques, which are connected with each other. The basic movements and *kokyu-ho* that I have explained so far are common to all techniques, and if you master them, you will naturally learn their details as you keep on with your training.

The Founder said that *dai-ikkyo* [first immobilization technique], which beginners first learn after entrance to dojo has the 'essence' of aikido. Techniques are classified as elementary, basic, and applied techniques for the sake of convenience so that students can learn them by stages, but, in the final analysis, every technique consists of basic movements and *kokyu-ho,* which means that every technique has the deepest secret and essence of aikido.

Tachi-waza, han-mi-han-dachi, and s*uwari-waza* [standing, sitting, and half-sitting-half- standing techniques] all use the very same body movements with minor differences in stance with relation to each position. If you find applied techniques or sitting techniques difficult, it means that something is wrong with your body movements and *kokyu-ho* even in basic techniques. Try to practice basic body movements and *kokyu-ho* properly without being too conscious of variations, and you will improve your skills in using a wide variety of techniques.

In the case of *buki-dori* [weapon-snatching techniques], in addition to posture, you also have to mind the position where you take control over your opponent (in consideration of the position of the blade) and suppress such feelings as fear and nervousness in dealing with your armed opponent, but the basic principle remains the same: you take a broad view of him/her opponent and make proper use of basic body movements and *kokyu-ho*.

Having said that, as long as we humans are not perfect and all different from each other, I admit that it is fairly difficult to practice any technique exactly the same way with any partner. Therefore, not only five-kyu beginners but six-dan, seven-dan black belts also keep practicing the same techniques, which are the basics and the essence at the same time. Those basic techniques you keep on practicing are all the same in form, but those performed by five-kyu students and high-rankers look totally different in terms of the degree of perfection.

Tight Training and Soft Training

The type of training focusing on the basics is sometimes called 'tight training'. Tight training does not mean straining yourself and exerting you powers fully, though, to be sure, it is not always easy to relaxing yourself in this type of training. On the other hand, proper relaxation is not possible just by letting your body go limp. You need some experience in letting go of superfluous strength. In tight training, you grip firmly but relax your joints. You can slow down if necessary, but what you need to do, whether you are *tori* or *uke*, is to make sure sensitively that your body is properly functioning in moving as well as in exerting strength.

After going through such training, then you move on to 'soft training'. It is a type of training in which you take turns in practicing techniques in a flow of movements, which is sometimes referred to as 'flow of *ki*-energy', without being too conscious of the function of strength and body movements. You do not just move around aimlessly but make reasonable and systematic movements smoothly. For techniques are generated from reasonable and systematic movements.

Some people say that it looks as though *uke* takes a jump of his/her own accord, but there is no fixed agreement concerning such a movement. *Tori* applies a technique on *uke*, who then

The author demonstrating the way his strength operates and transmits through his knife hands

takes a break-fall to protect his/her body. When *tori* moves to unbalance *uke*, the latter takes a self-protective break-fall without trying to stand firm or resist too much. This is the way a technique works and *tori* practices it properly. On the contrary, if *uke*, without being properly thrown off balance, jumps of his/her own accord to take a break-fall, *tori* cannot practice techniques properly.

You need to take turns to practice techniques properly, understanding each other, taking a proper stance, and feeling how effectively they are applied. At demonstration sessions as well, *uke* jumps on to the mat, not to show off the effectiveness of the techniques *tori* used, but to demonstrate proper ways to take break-falls when they are applied properly. They are not performing a strength contest or competition. It is impossible in aikido that *uke* should be thrown away without tori touching him/her. If it looked as if the impossible thing had happened, it simply means both *tori* and *uke* have not been properly trained.

Tight training does not mean straining yourself and compete stiffly with your partner, nor does soft training mean going limp in practicing techniques. Tight training is designed to sensitize you to the basics of aikido and lead you to soft training in which you practice flowing movements. Soft training is only possible after mastering the basics and will not work well if beginners try to join it. On the contrary, advanced students should not do away with tight training.

It sometimes happens that a beginner pairs up with an advanced student. In such a case, they adjust the tightness and softness of their training so that both of them can practice techniques properly. The advanced student thus relearns the basics and the beginner feels the softness of movements that is essential in aikido. Then both students improve their skills at their respective levels. This it the way I hope aikido training should go.

There Is No Completion in Technical Training

Dai-ikkyo, irimi-nage, and *shiho-nage* are three basic techniques all students learn right after starting aikido training. They are techniques in which irimi and *tenkan* movements and *kokyu-ho* are very simply combined together, but advanced students do not stop practicing them. Even those students of twenty or thirty years of training experience also practice them repeatedly.

Earlier on I said that your techniques reveal your life and experience. As time passes, we all change physically and mentally. Young people grow up and, from a certain point, grow old. Muscular strength weakens and joints stiffen; on the other hand, experience provides composure and relaxation. As a human body is changing every day, you need to practice techniques in consideration of your mental and physical conditions of the time. In short, you need to face your mind and body every time you practice aikido. There is no completion in technical training.

You get to know your renewed self and new techniques, as is also the case with your training partners. You can say, then, that an application of a technique is a once-in-a-lifetime experience and never replicated again. Although it is extremely challenging to keep practicing incomplete techniques, it is also a pleasant experience to refresh yourself and make new discoveries at every training session. This may be one of the reasons, in addition to the results of physical training, why experienced aikidoists tend to look younger than they really are.

There are well over a hundred techniques including throwing, throwing-and-grappling, and grappling techniques, with standing, half-sitting-half-standing, and sitting variations, multiplied by the number of attacking moves and front, back, and other body movements. In order to master all of them you need to practice them in a well-balanced way, but it will take several years, even if you do so every day, to acquire general skills in applying them. On top of that, there is no telling how long it will take you to become able to practice any of them in the same way with any training partner.

Some people, simply aiming at the acquisition of a first dan, stop coming to dojo once the aim has been attained. However, training starts anew for you from that point to work further on the basics. In long years of training, you practice techniques successfully sometimes and unsuccessfully at other times. In that sense, nobody has 'special techniques' at which he or she is particularly good.

Why We Keep on with Training

Training lasts for one's lifetime. Then, why do we keep on with training? After entering dojo, you keep practicing techniques in turns, sometimes feeling refreshed in moving actively and sweating all over and sometimes finding pleasure in making friends with people from all walks of life. Some people may keep practicing techniques, aspiring to be better at them and get to higher grades, or to learn many other techniques. These are concrete aims of training, which drive you on to further learning.

However, I truly hope that you will not keep on training aikido just for the sake of acquiring skills or enjoying it as a pastime. We should not forget the ideals of our predecessors who elevated those 'martial skills' of killing and hurting opponents to 'budo' designed to help the sound development of mind and body and passed its tradition down to the present day. The Founder's 'Guidelines for Practicing Aikido' stipulate that aikido should aim to 'create citizens of integrity through mental and physical training'. 'Citizens of integrity' are those people who are always sincere to anyone. I hope, therefore, that all aikido students realize in their respective social lives, the spirit underlying all the training methods I have explained so far.

'Be sincere to anyone.' It is easier said than done. We all have likes and dislikes concerning people around us. It will be easy to be sincere to others when you feel fine physically and emotionally, but how about when you feel otherwise? You constantly experience many things in your social life, ups and downs in your work or family life, which may sometimes make you emotionally unstable or even unreasonable. Such changes in your feelings and mental states convey themselves delicately through your hands and skin.

Far be it from me to say that you can survive them all if you are practicing aikido, but I really wish you to acquire the strength by means of aikido training to contain yourself and stay sincere at the time of trouble. It is also the strength to keep your composure face to face with someone, who, if recognized as an enemy, would put you on full alert. If you acquire it, you can cope with any situation or any type of people, because without competition you are the invincible one, invulnerable to any harm in the world. If asked whether I have attained this state of perfect invincibility, I am afraid I have to answer 'no, not yet'; I still have a long way to go.

Even the Founder said, 'I'll keep on with aikido training for the rest of my life'. He also said, 'I have no disciple, but I have a lot of fellow trainees'. I will also keep on training in order to be a 'citizen of integrity'. I am going the same way with you all. There is no completion in technical training, as I said, and no end to the journey. The above-mentioned state may be something unattainable in one's lifetime. Just a little bit of aikido training will not lead you to the perfect understanding of the art, but your strenuous efforts to get there are extremely valuable by themselves. The ideal of aikido, though unattainable, is always there, to be sure, and we all keep on going towards it, aspiring to get there. This is the Way itself.

Aikido Has No Contest

'Do you not fight in a contest situation?' is a question posed to me fairly often. This is a little bit tricky question, because, before the discussion of fighting or not fighting, we do not have any contest from the beginning.

In aikido training, *tori* (the one who applies techniques) and *uke* (the other on whom they are applied) take turns. You apply techniques at one time and have them applied on at another, which means that you spend half of your training time taking break-falls. By becoming a target of techniques and taking break-falls, you learn not only how to protect yourself but also many more things. For example, you learn how the force of *tori* is transmitted to you. It is also a very good opportunity to reflect on your own techniques. In so doing, you grow more respectful to your partners. While keeping on with your training, you also learn the importance of harmonizing with them and move on to higher stages of physical and mental training.

The aim of aikido training is not to be a better aikidoist than others or win a competition but to learn techniques, develop yourself and elevate each other mentally and physically. We have neither contest nor any system for considering the level of skills in grading or competition. I am not saying, let me hasten to add, that aikido is superior to other sports with systems for competition. In those sports you also discipline yourself, keep on training, with due respect to judges, instructors, opponents, or teammates (in the case of team sports), play fair, work hard in sound rivalry with your opponents, and finally praise each other's performances. What you experience in those sports will be wonderful, and they have a lot of values which are acknowledged by a great many people in the world.

There is neither contests nor competitive games in aikido. If you feel competitive and vie with your opponents for physical strength or better skills, or if you are disrespectful to your master or training partners, not self-disciplined enough, or not willing to improve yourself, what you practice should not be called aikido. What is important to acknowledge in others is neither superiority nor inferiority but difference. What is more important to consider when you are working on something is not what to do but how to do it. That is to say, it all depends on how you look at what you are working on. I will not discuss the values of aikido in comparison with something else.

The proper way to improve yourself is not to vie for something but polish what you think is good in you into something better. All I am going to do is to keep teaching aikido, which I know and firmly believe is a wonderful martial art. I will do it the very same way that I demonstrate techniques at training sessions. I just keep showing what is good and hope good results will follow.

In 1990, NHK Educational TV broadcast a programme on aikido in the 'Sports Classes' series. It enjoyed a favourable reception from the viewers, and Educational TV broadcast another programme on aikido (for the intermediate learners) in the following year, which was followed by some more aikido-related programmes. This is a good sign to show, I believe, that there are potentially a great number of people who want to learn aikido now.

As a matter of fact, Long before NHK brought to us the proposal concerning the 'Sports Classes' programme, I once visited NHK, bringing an aikido handbook with me, to suggest the possibility of making an educational TV programme on aikido. At that time my suggestion was turned down without any serious consideration simply because Aikikai was not a member of the Japan Sport Association.

We got a similar response when I explained aikido to some people at the Ministry of Education (now Ministry of Education, Culture, Sports, Science and Technology [MEXT]). Today, most of the Japanese martial-art organizations with corporate status have competitive systems except aikido, and they suggested a couple of times that aikido should also suggest a competitive system. Of course, we have continued to respond by saying 'aikido has no contest'. Now, it reminds me how time has changed to see the MEXT taking aikido into serious consideration in relation to lifelong education.

Asia University put aikido into its regular curriculum of physical education in 1964. The Founder himself went to the university and demonstrated his skills. After that, the Department of Martial Arts of Tokai University, International Budo University, Nippon Sport Science University, Kogakkan University, and Nihon University also introduced aikido into their regular curricula of physical education, and we have sent instructors from the Hombu Dojo. In 2012, when budo became

The author teaching an aikido class at Kogakkan University

a compulsory subject of physical education in the curriculum of junior high school, aikido was adopted as one of the elective martial-art subjects, though not by many schools. This suggests that aikido, even without contest or competitive games, has been acknowledged as a suitable subject for the mental and physical development of young people.

Aikido is not designed to hold your opponents down with physical strength or techniques. Instead, it reconciles conflicts in perfect harmony with them. It was completed as a modern martial art that transcends all conflicts. I truly believe that the postwar development of aikido has been based on this aspect of the art. The peaceful idea of aikido has something to do with the Founder's faith in the deities in Kumano. Our family legend has it that he was born owing to the divine power of the Kumano Hongu Shrine. Since my great grandparents' children before him were all girls, they went to the Hongu Shrine many times to ask for the birth of a boy. I heard that the Founder was a gift from the god of the shrine.

Kumano worship originated in nature worship and, later incorporating Buddhism into itself, became a syncretic religion. One of the reasons why Kumano was registered as a World Heritage, as I heard, was that its religion was generous enough to accept other religions without any conflict. It is not surprising that Kumano worship, starting as nature worship in close contact with nature in Kumano, had some influence on the spirit of aikido. I believe that it is a spirit that attracts not only the Japanese but also other people in the world and has a role to play in realizing world peace.

The Japanese Spirit

Let me digress here to mention recent lawsuits in Japan, which are increasing in number, as I hear, almost to match those in Western countries. News shows report many incidents which suggest that Japanese people are becoming less generous to others' mistakes and drawbacks and overly critical about them. As Japan has been more globalized, experiencing new things, and the sense of values and ethical views of its society have changed over time, there now seem to be an increasing number of people who overtly express their emotions or take actions, which might have been restrained only a generation ago. We Japanese used to consider it the greatest disgrace to trouble other people. Now, such a sense of shame seems to have considerably weakened.

True, in modern society we may be required to make strict rules and assert our rights based on them, and it is partly a good thing. However, the downside is that people are becoming more self-centred and less capable of controlling their intense emotions such as anger, hatred, jealousy, and grief. I fear that the idea of respecting each other is going out of date. In order to construct a peaceful society, we need to live in harmony with other people in the spirit of 'live and let live', though we do not have to go so far as to force ourselves to understand or be friends with those people who have totally different ideas from ours or who we do not like.

At the time of the Great East Japan Earthquake, public order was not greatly disturbed, even though there were minor incidents of stockpiling, or thefts and burglaries under the cover of general confusions. Evacuation sites were kept clean, and, when relief items were delivered to them, evacuees queued up orderly so that items might be evenly distributed. Few people acted in a self-centred way, and many people around the world praised the way Japanese people cared about other people in time of trouble.

Even in our ordinary lives, commuters line up at the platform without being told to do so by anybody and, when a train arrives, they wait to see if anyone is getting off before they get on the train. We stand on one side of the escalator to keep the other side available for the people in a hurry. These habits are some of the good signs to show that the traditional ethical principle of 'live and let live' is still working in our society. Aikido is also based on such a principle Japanese people have long inherited, and this is presumably the reason why it has gained worldwide acceptance.

The author's votive performance at the Aiki Shrine

At the Aiki Shrine that the Founder raised, a spirit-consoling service for the Founder and the second Doshu is held on April the 29th every year with nearly 1500 worshippers inside and outside Japan.

The author having audience of Pope Francis I in 2016

Recently we have an increasing number of newcomers to dojo who have already had a preliminary knowledge about aikido. This suggests that an increasing number of people support the ideals of aikido; that many people recognize anew the importance of respecting and caring about others rather than competing with them to gain a victory or show how strong they are. What is appreciated here has been developed in the long history of Japan. Japanese people have long cultivated land, grown rice, reaped rice plants, and celebrated a good harvest every year. In so doing we have developed a culture in which special values are placed on living and working together with other people. We also inherited the spirit of respecting and caring about people. It has also found its way into the aikido principle of putting yourself in your opponent's shoes.

In times of trouble, we have endeavoured to find ways to

solve them in harmonious collaboration with each other. That endeavour has made the present society working. Out of this long tradition of harmonious endeavour, I think, emerged aikido naturally. The ideals of aikido then have attracted many people in Japan and further many people all over the world.

After the Repetition of Forms Your Originality Starts Shining

Let me explain more in detail the 'training methods unique to aikido'.

Aikido training is generally classified as *kata-geiko* [formal training]. '*Kata-geiko*' is a useful terminology for explaining the type of training adopted by many of the old Japanese martial arts. In martial arts there are also a training method called '*randori* [free practice]', in which you apply techniques rather freely in practical movements, and a more contest-based one, but aikido adopts neither of them.

In aikido, you first observe your instructor's demonstration of a model technique and then practice it repeatedly. This method may be generally classified as '*kata-geiko*', but neither the Founder nor Kisshomaru the second Doshu used the term. Kisshomaru the second Doshu told me that the Founder himself had used the term '*ki-gata*' instead.

In aikido training, trainees cannot imitate the technique the instructor demonstrated exactly the same way. They are different from each other in terms of physical construction and abilities, and placed in a different condition every time they practice a technique, and therefore cannot move exactly

The author standing with Kisshomaru the second Doshu
with the Founder's bust on low relief in between

the same way as their instructor. Instructors also differ from each other. In the Hombu Dojo there are more than thirty instructors, who do not take charge of the same classes every day. You will see them demonstrate the selfsame technique in slightly different ways, for example, in the way they step forward to throw their opponents off balance. Their differences emerge naturally as a result of their respective experiencces of training aikido for a long time.

Aikido techniques look rather different, I have heard some people say, depending on the instructor who demonstrates them. When you start practicing the 'basics', you may wonder what the 'basics' are. This is a legitimate question. My answer is that, just as we all have different physical constructions, characters, and views of life, so instructors have different ways of moving in demonstrating techniques. However, let me hasten to add, they are not demonstrating different techniques; they are doing the same thing at the very basic level.

I would advise aikido students not to problematize their instructors' differences in demonstrating techniques but to accept them with an open mind as their characteristics and observe their model techniques. Teachers are not expecting all their students to be able to do exactly the same thing as they did, and it is true of all kinds of teaching and learning. It is not wise to have a fixed idea about 'the right way' to do something, and, after all, aikido should not be reduced down to a set of fixed forms. Having said that, you should not deviate too much from the basics.

You need to utilize basic body movements and *kokyu-ryoku* developed through *kokyu-ho* to apply such techniques as *ikkyo, irimi-nage*, and *shiho-nage*. I want all of you to go through this process of basic training. Everything resides in the basics.

What looks odd or eccentric right before your eyes does not last long, no matter how striking it is. It is my duty to make sure that everyday training should be prioritized and to keep practicing what has been passed down from the Founder through Kisshomaru the second Doshu to me.

Observe carefully your teacher's demonstration of techniques and keep practicing them steadily, and you will internalize the experience in you and make your originality shine out. This training method of observation and repetition may

The author demonstrating a model technique in front of observant participants in one of his training sessions; students all learn the same basics and keep on training until individual characteristics naturally emerge.

be considered a formalistic and depersonalizing method of simply copying what your teacher does. This is a great misunderstanding. We humans are all different from each other. Even if you observe the same demonstration and practice techniques in the same way, your movements and techniques are slightly different from others' reflecting what you were born with. No matter how faithful you try to be to a model, your own nature reveals itself in the way you practice it. Therefore, you cannot be an exact copy of your teacher, even if he or she tries very hard to make you one, just as brothers and sisters, who are born of the same parents, live in the same house, eat the same food, and go to the same school, still grow to be different children with different personalities.

Originality is not what you can force out of yourself or create with the conscious intention of 'being different from others'. If you practice aikido steadily according to its basics and principles, your techniques naturally represent something of you. That 'something', shining out of you, filled with enduring strength and confidence acquired through steady practice of the basics, is nothing other than your 'originality' in the truest sense of the word. Nothing takes shape without basic principles, and your originality comes out after your long experiences of strenuous training. You cannot acquire outstanding skills out of nothing. You keep on training for a long time, and as a result you will find yourself equipped with your own originality.

In order to make this happen, instructors need to teach the basics carefully and to evaluate the diversity of students that emerges out of the fundamental framework of training. It is not a good idea to try very hard to 'develop students' originality' or 'let them practice their own techniques'. All they need to do is simply to make sure that basic training should go on.

All You Need to Do to Improve Your Aikido Skills Is to Practice Aikido

One of the tendencies after the war is that some masters have incorporated training methods for wielding a sword or stave into some part of their aikido training. This sometimes causes misunderstanding.

Morihei Ueshiba the Founder sometimes used a wooden

sword, stave, or even spear by way of an explanatory tool. He also learned many traditional martial arts. Those masters might have seen as disciples what the Founder learned and tried in the process of studying martial arts and creating aikido. However, the Founder often said, 'All disciples here are my disciples. They all came here to practice aikido. ... All you need to do to improve your aikido skills is to practice aikido. We don't need the help of any other martial arts.'

There are also other masters who explain aikido in reference to Zen, but neither the Founder nor Kisshomaru the second Doshu ever practiced Zen. Nor they recommended Zen meditation to aikido students. Although the Founder was a disciple of Onisaburo Deguchi of Oomoto and studied Shinto, *Kojiki*, and *kotodama* [the soul of language], he never forced his disciples to practice anything other than aikido itself. Nor did he ever advise any of his students to practice using a sword or stave, convert to his faith, or study *kotodama*. It is perfectly all right for aikido masters to practice anything other than aikido for their own training, but it is not a good idea to strongly recommend their disciples to practice other martial arts. They should not forget that they claim to be and are qualified as aikido instructors and are actually teaching aikido. You can try many different martial arts to borrow their good points, which, however, can be your own only after practicing each of them for a long time. You need to keep practicing one thing to master it. Aikido, originated by the Founder and systematized after the war by Kisshomaru the second Doshu, is self-sufficient. You need to practice no other martial arts or philosophical teachings to understand and be good at aikido.

Before, during and right after the war, there were many

aikido students who had already learned other martial arts before starting aikido training. After the war we have had an increasing number of students without any such experiences. In order to make aikido accessible to the general public, Kisshomaru the second Doshu systematized it in consideration of the safety of physical training so that any aikido students, young and old, men and women, can understand and practice it, starting from warming-up exercises, moving on to basic movements, then to further technical training. The Founder originated aikido after practicing and studying many things, and the second Doshu systematized the methodology for physical and technical training. We should not forget that we are practicing aikido in this context.

Many of the Founder's high-ranking disciples who learned aikido under his tutelage before and during the war had already been distinguished martial artists. These predecessors of aikido do not know the pains Kisshomaru the second Doshu took in systematizing techniques and training methods. Before and during the war the nomenclature of aikido techniques was not so firmly established as today. There was a term '*irimi*', but the expressions '*omote* [front]' and '*ura* [back]' techniques were not used at that time. This is quite natural, because the Founder did not explain his techniques closely but simply demonstrate them on impulse and encourage his students to do the same. No wonder there was no systematic terminology. It is not too much to say that techniques themselves were different depending on the time the Founder showed them.

The guidelines for the promotion test also have been elaborated. Before they were presented, the Founder gave licenses to his disciples at his discretion based on his

The Founder originated aikido, and Kisshomaru the second Doshu systematized it into its present style so that anyone can practice it.

observation of their daily training. Now that we have the guidelines, which stipulate the techniques the examinees are expected to perform and the number of days they need to spend in training to be promoted, anyone who is qualified as an aikido master (six dan and upwards) in any part of Japan can conduct a promotion text on his or her own. The reason why the masters at the Hombu Dojo and I always emphasize the importance of contextualizing aikido in history, with reference to what happened in our lineal succession of the art—from the Founder through Kisshomaru the second Doshu to me—is that the present aikido is firmly based on its history.

Perform Normally at Examination and Demonstration

One of the major occasions to examine what you have achieved in aikido training is an examination for promotion. After training aikido for the number of days stipulated for promotion to the grade you want, you are qualified to demonstrate your techniques in front of your examiner (master). You also need to show your skills in taking proper break-falls at the stipulated techniques.

A promotion test is not designed to fail you but to examine what you have achieved in training. From the viewpoint of examinees, it is not what they take to be promoted to their target grades but an opportunity to see how their skills have been improved. Before the war there was no examination; after the war, as aikido got more popularized, an examination system was introduced to provide each student with an immediate goal at every stage of their training. I am not quite sure about entrance examinations, but normal in-school examinations are not necessarily designed to grade students but to see if they mastered what they have learned in the classroom.

If you can demonstrate what you have practiced, you are unlikely to fail. Do not get self-conscious and stiffen nor try to demonstrate techniques better than you have done in daily training, which after all is impossible. I would strongly advise you to perform normally.

The same principle applies to the occasions where you demonstrate techniques in the presence of a large company.

The author heading towards the centre of the hall to give his special demonstration

Aikido techniques used to be secretly practiced only among the Founder's disciples and, therefore, had never been demonstrated in the presence of other people until the 30s of the Showa period, when demonstration meetings were regularized for the purpose of promotion of aikido. At first, demonstrations were given only by the Founder and instructors, but later the policy for organizing demonstration meetings changed so that ordinary members can look forward to them as opportunities to demonstrate their skills and make sure of what they have practiced. Situations of demonstration meetings are rather different from those of promotion tests— the venues are much larger and the number of spectators far greater—but again my advice is the same: perform normally; do as you always do.

Having said that, it is easier said than done; no matter how hard we try to 'perform normally' or 'do as we always do', we tend to get nervous on those special occasions. In order to get over tension, here again we need to keep on with our training, technical as well as mental. I would advise ordinary members, who are not specialists like masters or instructors, to understand demonstration meetings as 'opportunities to make sure of what you have practiced' and enjoy them.

You do not keep training for the purpose of taking a test or joining a demonstration meeting. Training itself is the aim of your training. Even if you cannot perform at a test or demonstration as skillfully as you have expected, it is not the end of your aikido. It should be understood as another challenge for you, and all you have to do is to keep training to surmount it.

Can We Get Strong by Practicing Aikido?

This is a question posed to me from time to time. I guess there are some people who are interested in learning aikido to acquire skills in self-defense.

Supposing someone suddenly attacks you, is it possible to keep him or her under control as you have done in your daily aikido practice? This depends more on how much aikido practice you have done rather than whether you have practiced aikido or not. It is impossible to suppose all the possible situations of the attack in advance. In what kind of place in which part of the world will it take place? It may take place when you are asleep or in those situations where you are injured or have a small child in tow. You have no idea whether the attacker has any weapon, When it comes to that, it will be more a matter of caution or risk awareness than martial arts used in self-defense.

My quick advice is: stay away from dangerous places and keep clear of danger. Whether or not you can keep your opponent under control depends entirely on the power relationship between two of you. It is rather more realistic to try to make a proper decision to ensure safety depending on the situation in which you are placed. If you prioritize your safety, it is wiser to take a good look at your opponent(s), take a proper distance from the danger, leave the place, or call for help. If you try to beat or control your opponent(s), there arises a combat situation; if you try to protect yourself or avoid an unnecessary combat, you can make a proper judgment. In this respect, aikido training will be of great help to you, for you will acquire an unprejudiced attitude towards people and things, which will naturally make you more cautious and careful enough to stay away from any danger or combat.

Many people ask me, 'Can we be strong by practicing aikido?' What does it mean to be 'strong'? My guess is that they want to know whether they can surpass others in physical strength in combat. By beating someone in fighting or wrestling the winner can prove one kind of strength. I understand that some people who start budo training aspire to acquire this kind of 'strength'. It may be a human instinct to crave for it. It does not make much sense, however, to ask whether aikidoists can beat any other martial artists or not. It presumably depends on the physical abilities of individuals and has little bearing on the type of martial arts they practice. Or, what happens if someone attacks you with a knife or tries to shoot you with a gun? When it comes to that, it is almost meaningless to ask which martial art is 'stronger' than others.

What every aikido student should aspire to acquire is the kind of moral strength that works extensively in a wide range of human activities. A lot of troubles happen in our jobs and human relationships. You have to cope with explosive situations in a well-balanced way to avoid conflicts; collaborate in harmony with other people in pushing things forward in spite of differences in tastes, ideas, opinions, ages, characters, and walks of life; and keep on doing one thing steadily. These are the ways in which you need to be strong in your lives. You need to keep on training in order to be strong not only physically but also mentally. It would be almost meaningless to practice budo today unless you have a place outside dojo where you can work with other people as a good citizen.

What Begins with Courtesy Ends with Courtesy

There are a lot of parents who want their children to learn good manners by means of aikido training. What I want those parents to understand is that children learn manners not because they make bows and behave politely at aikido lessons but because they learn to be grateful to others through aikido training.

Aikido students bow to the front of the dojo on entering it,

We bow to the front of the dojo to express our gratitude to our predecessors and the dojo itself before starting training.

leaving it, at the beginning and end of training. At the front of each dojo is hung a portrait of or a brush calligraphy by the Founder, sometimes together with hangings connected with the founder or head of the dojo. We bow to the front of the dojo to pay respect to our predecessors who laid the foundations of aikido, to those who provide the training hall for us, and the training hall itself.

We also make a bow to our instructors and training partners, for we cannot practice aikido alone. By doing that we express our respect and gratitude to those who teach aikido to us as well as others who help us learn aikido. Without respect and gratitude, aikido training loses its basis. We bow not because it is one of the formalities of martial arts but because we are truly grateful and respectful to them. This is the core of courtesy [rei].

Aikido today is practiced enthusiastically all over the world, where there are many people of different faiths, including those who disapprove of idolatry. To those people I make a point of explaining that what we do at dojo is not related to any religion but more concerned with manners and etiquette. As regards the details of those manners, we do not have any fixed rules in aikido, though some people are particular about the order of placing your hands on the mat or that of legs to bring forward to stand up, or about what you are expected to behave in samurai-style ceremonies or the tea ceremony. We take a *kiza* posture [kneel on toes] in standing up or sitting down, but it is not a formality; we simply do it because it makes our movement much more smooth. When you take a proper posture and move naturally, the whole flow of movements looks beautiful. Courtesy lies not in formalities but in your heart.

Do Not Ask for Immediate Results

Manners and etiquette, health, and physical fitness are some of the things that many students of aikido try to acquire through training. However, they become your own as a result of assiduous training. They are not something you can get immediately if you practice aikido.

Right after you start aikido training, you keep on throwing your partners and being thrown by them for one hour in one session. You get thrown, roll on the mat, stand up, and get thrown again. These movements are not familiar to you in daily lives and therefore considerably fatiguing. You suffer greatly from muscular and other bodily pains for the first couple of months. Then, if you successfully get through this painful experience, you get accustomed to lessons, get acquainted with

The author presenting a certificate to the representative of participants in All Japan Training Meeting for Boys and Girls

fellow students at your dojo, and enjoy keeping on with training for a considerable length of time. However, it also happens that many people stop short of reaching that stage.

Although aikido aims to create 'citizens of integrity', what we do to attain the aim is simply to practice aikido techniques. As long as I am an aikido instructor myself, all I do at dojo is to see that learning and training are properly going. I do not necessarily preach in the style of precepts about how we should all live in this world. Do not aim at some immediate benefit; just try to see retrospectively what you have achieved through training, and you can enjoy your training much longer. Nothing is more gratifying to me than your retrospective observation that aikido has been worth practicing.

As I wrote earlier on, 'what to do' is not as important as 'how to do it'. I truly hope that you will keep on aikido training

The author giving a lecture at one of his overseas training sessions, where participants are enthusiastically keeping on with their own training

at your own pace without asking for immediate results. Even if you increase the intensity and frequency of training haphazardly, you cannot get immediate effects as you expect. After all, you cannot keep on with excessive training. You need to take time to develop yourself technically, physically, and mentally.

You may hit a slump, unable to practice techniques as successfully as you wish. You may even want to quit aikido. No matter how much bitterness and pain you may experience on each occasion, I would advise you to keep on with your training by looking forward to your future improvement. This is what *do* [the Way] is all about. When you look back on the way you have come, you will realize that you are heading in the right direction. The realization will make you feel confident and easy. Then, it may further develop into kindness and respect to other people. I said earlier that there is no completion to techniques, and a similar thing can be said about the 'results' of training, which may not appear in a clear-cut way. The Way may be the process itself in which you keep going, taking one step at a time.

Respect to Predecessors

There are many young people who have practiced aikido for long years and older people who have not practiced it so much, starting their training later in life. I make a point of advising young instructors, who have just started their teaching career in Aikikai, to teach with due respect to those older people who have seen more of the world than they. On the other hand, aikido students need to pay respect to their instructor at training sessions, even if he or she is much younger than they. Otherwise, training falls apart.

I guess it is also true of society in general. When many people are involved in one project, it would be better to acknowledge what is good in other people—experience, ability, and other merits—and collaborate with each other with respect. I also have a similar experience. When I started my career as an aikido instructor, I took charge of classes where there were many students who were older than I and richer in social and life experiences, and I learned a lot from them. We all can develop ourselves by taking a modest and respectful attitude towards other people and trying to learn from them.

There are a variety of first-dan students. Some have excellent athletic and physical abilities and, therefore, master skills in a very short period of time, which, of course, is a good thing. On the other hand, there are others who have acquired a first dan after many years of steady training. Although those two groups of people are standing at the same technical level, they are different in terms of the number of training sessions they have participated in and the length of time they have spent in training. One of the good points about aikido training is that experienced students can naturally guide others simply by training with them and functioning as *uke* to them.

Experiences never fail to reveal themselves in training. We all lose a lot of physical strength as we grow old, but what we achieve through training will surely be estimable and become part of us. I hope I can conduct daily lessons in such a way that training experiences should be duly appreciated. In my aikido classes I sometimes see students being competitive with their partners or trying to apply techniques forcefully. As they keep on with their training, I hope, they will learn that there is more to aikido than technical training.

As you grow old, you may sometimes find it painful to bring a grappling technique to an end in a proper sitting posture or apply a half-sitting-half-standing technique. As long as aikido consists largely of physical training, you have to face a decline in stamina. Nevertheless, you need to try your best in the present condition and keep on with your training to improve yourself.

Now that forty-six years have passed since I started substantial aikido training, I also have pains sometimes in my lower back and legs and have lost much of the explosive power I used to have when young. Still I have been much more improved than that time thanks to what I have achieved through long years of

The author demonstrating a technique at a training session in an international aikido meeting; extensive training with a variety of people is a prerequisite for your technical development.

training with a variety of people. With a well-balanced mixture of abilities to discern other's skills, physical construction, and character, harmonize with his/her movements, keep a proper distance from him/her, and judge the right timing for moving my body, I believe myself to be a better aikidoist than I used to be.

Even as you grow old and lose some of the skills you used to have, you gain more and are improved in overall ability. Only an accumulation of regular training will lead you to that stage. You will not be able to get immediate effects of training, but if you keep on training with a strong will, you will surely find yourself much improved in retrospect.

The Tradition of Aikido

My Grandfather: Morihei Ueshiba

I remember it was around the time when I was a second or third grader at elementary school. I was so hungry right after coming back from school that I grilled rice cakes on the brazier in the living room and ate them with bean flouer and *nori*. Then, my grandfather suddenly came into the room, and I handed him a rice cake saying, 'Here you are'. He replied, 'You are a good boy' ,and received it from my hand.

He is my grandfather by blood and the Founder of aikido at the same time. On many occasions I saw him treated reverentially by adults around him. I had a vague understanding that he is very special to other people. When he was with his disciples, there was a tacit understanding that children should stay away from them. He was a grandfather to take to but somewhat unapproachable at the same time. He was not the type of person who holds out his hand to invite us to play with him, and on my part I kept a modest distance from him.

This ambivalence might have come from the difference between his positions at dojo and at home. Today the distance between instructors and students is much shorter than the Founder's days when there was a great difference in position and a clear line of demarcation between masters and their disciples. After all, he is not just a master but also the Founder of aikido.

At that time the main house of the Ueshibas was connected to the dojo, where there were many other people than his disciples. I could not make up to him in the presence of those

Morihei Ueshiba the Founder of aikido and an affectionate grandfather to the author at home; right: the Founder with the author in his childhood; left: the Founder departing for Hawaii and the author (centre)

people, of course, but he really was 'Grandpa' when watching television alone with me. When I patted him on the head, saying, 'Grandpa's head is very slick', he reportedly said with a smile on his face, 'This boy is the only person that pats this old man's head'. He was a fan of samurai films, and we would watch them together. I still remember the time when I was enjoying sumo wresting with my friends who came to my house. He came to us, saying, 'Let me join you' ,and joined us in sumo wresting.

In the mid-thirties of the Showa era, when I entered elementary school, my grandfather spent two-thirds of a year in Tokyo and one-third in Iwama. During such long holidays as a summer vacation, I sometimes visited him in Iwama. My grandfather, though in his seventies at that time, was even carrying for himself a heavy stone mortar for rice-cake pounding. Just like a man of the Meiji period, he had gone through those times in which many daily activities—farm work, drawing water, wood chopping, etc.—contributed to physical training.

At that time, my father took charge of regular classes at the Hombu Dojo. When the Founder was in Tokyo, he sometimes presented himself at the Dojo and, after demonstrating his exquisite skills or talking about the spirit of aikido for about half an hour, leave the place, saying, 'For the rest I leave everything to you, Kisshomaru'.

When I took part in a morning session as a child, my grandfather once demonstrated some techniques. All I understood at that time was that they were just splendid. Looking back on his demonstration at that time, I think he had a power to embrace and attract his opponent. His face and penetrating eyes at that time were not my grandfather's but the Founder's. The occasion on which I was particularly impressed by his special power was the demonstration meeting held at the Hibiya Public Hall in 1964. Two thousand people who came to the venue to take a look at the Founder's art of aikido were glued to his every move and embraced in one atmosphere. Then I thought, 'Oh, Grandpa is great; he is a true genius'.

When I was a third-year student at high school, a few days before my grandfather's death, Mr. Hiroshi Arakawa (former hitting coach of the Yomiuri Giants and six-dan aikidoist) came to my house with Mr. Sadaharu Oh, his favourite disciple, to inquire after my grandfather's health. I was looking at their

The Founder teaching a class at the Hombu Dojo circa the mid-thirties in the Showa era

meeting, thinking in wonderment that my grandfather must be a great man to have such a famous visitor as Mr. Oh. Then, my grandfather took a look at Mr. Oh's face and said, 'Well, you have the physiognomy of a grandmaster'. I was extremely impressed that he spontaneously tried to flatter and please his visitors in spite of his poor physical condition.

He belonged to the older generation and was therefore conservative in some aspects. After the war, we started enjoying a lot of sports broadcast and witnessed an increasing number of women participating in sports, but he did not necessarily approve of the way women looked in TV sports programmes. When we were watching a game of women's volleyball on TV, he disapprovingly said, 'I just don't understand why these girls have to do this ...'. When I quickly responded by saying, 'But, Grandpa, there are many women practicing aikido', he stammered, 'Aikido is an exception'. He seemed to think it ungraceful for girls to have their bare legs uncovered.

It is normal practice today for an Aikikai student to begin to wear a hakama when he or she is promoted to a first dan, but a female student is allowed to wear it when promoted to a third kyu. This is not a fixed rule but a custom that has naturally emerged out of tacit understanding among Aikikai people.

When you take part in a training session, you straighten up in a *hakama*. Before the war everyone wore a *hakama* to practice aikido. The standard color of an aikido *hakama* now is black or dark blue, but a white *iai hakama* was also used in those days. During the war Japanese people suffered a severe shortage of goods, and even after the war not all students could afford to get a *hakama*. Therefore, from the 20s to 30s of the Showa era, students were allowed to participate in training sessions without wearing it.

When the popularity of aikido was taking root in universities, there arose a general understanding that it was too much to require every incoming member of aikido clubs to purchase an expensive *hakama* in addition to a minimum set of training wear; hence the custom of waiting for a promotion to a first dan before wearing a *hakama*. As aikido got more popularized, the general practice of wearing a *hakama* to mark a promotion to a first dan spread into ordinary members of Aikikai.

My Father: Kisshomaru Ueshiba

My father married my mother, Sakuko, in 1948 and moved with her for safety to Iwama where my grandparents lived. While helping them with farm work and leading a self-sufficient life, he assembled the local youth to teach aikido. In the same year my elder brother was born. Thinking of the boy's future, my father decided to put an end to his life there and go to Tokyo to establish himself in the world. Then he left behind my brother and my mother, who was doing badly after her confinement, and went to Tokyo to settle in the dojo in Wakamatsu-cho (now the Hombu Dojo of Aikido), totally dilapidated and exposed to rain at that time, to embark on the reconstruction of aikido. It was in 1949.

He first resumed regular training. The Founder came to Tokyo only a few times a month and there were only seven or eight students. Since it was almost impossible to earn a living by teaching aikido in those days, my father had no choice other than to find a job elsewhere and entered the Osaka Trading Company (now Mizuho Securities) with the help of one of his acquaintances. I think he was the only new hire with a kid.

I was born in 1951. The main dojo (former Hombu Dojo) was connected to the main house of the Ueshibas and was to me an extension of my playroom. I still remember playing in the dojo when I was three or four, and one of my old photographs shows me riding a tricycle there.

Neither the Founder nor my father told me to practice aikido, but I took part in training in dojo when I entered elementary

The author with his father, Kisshomaru the second Doshu, circa the late 20s of the Showa era

school. In those days there was no aikido wear for children, and I wore a small kendo wear which my father wore in his childhood. I still remember my father's face shining with joy.

When I was five years old and not yet an elementary-school pupil, it so happened that, when my father was about to leave to go to his company, there was no other adult in the house where we normally had someone around. My father did not want to leave his small boy alone and decided to take me to his company. I handed raisins to each of the employers instead of business cards, and became the centre of their attention. I ate lunch with employers at the staff canteen and, if I remember rightly, took some sleep in the afternoon. Things moved slowly and peacefully in those days.

What I did not realize as a child was that my father was more devoted to aikido than anyone else. He never asked anyone to take care of the training at the Hombu Dojo. He thanked Heaven for protecting the Hombu Dojo from fire and kept teaching morning classes himself. Indeed, he continued to teach them at the Hombu Dojo as long as he was its head. It

The Hombu Dojo was connected to the main house of the Ueshiba's until 1968 when the new building was completed, and many of our family photographs were taken before the Hombu Dojo;
right: the author with his parents and brother circa the early 30s of the Showa era

might not be a 'great achievement' to be praised, but as his successor I would really like to salute him for doing one thing till the end. He did many things to promote aikido—sending live-in disciples to universities as voluntary instructors, persuading the Founder to approve of public demonstration, starting publication projects, inventing training methods to be practiced at centres for cultural education, etc.—but never wavered in his belief.

As times change, society changes. While making aikido more accessible to the general public accordingly, he was determined to keep the unchangeable spirit of aikido as it had been. Considering the drastic change of Japanese people's sense of values and a trend of the times, he had to systematize and explain aikido, one of the traditional Japanese arts, and increase the number of aikido students. He had to face a mountain of difficult problems including the dilemma of reconciling necessary changes in training methods with the unchangeable do spirit.

It is the duty of the Ueshiba family, I think, to protect the Founder's art of aikido and hand it down to the next generation wholeheartedly without being distracted by considerations of immediate loss and gain. My father inherited the spirit and techniques of the Founder's art and at the same time, sensitizing himself to the changes of the times, embarked on reforming the whole system of aikido in order to meet the demands of society. What he did will be most simply summed up as the modernization and popularization of aikido, but his efforts to protect and extend the Way of aikido were too great to express in words.

My father devoted his life to organizing the Founder's art of aikido, which had not necessarily been easy for ordinary people to understand, into an understandable system and making it available to the general public. In order to attain his aim, he wrote many books. In my childhood I saw him sitting at the desk after the day's training sessions at dojo and writing for a long time and thought that it must be a very demanding job. After these assiduous efforts he established aikido anew as a practice-based methodology for the sound development of mind and body.

In consideration of the future development of aikido, he also devoted himself to teaching university students. His efforts at

Kisshomaru the second Doshu reading a book on martial skills, absorbed in deep thought; he devoted his life to the promotion and development of aikido, and his achievements are highly evaluated inside and outside Japan.

promoting it bore fruit in the growth of the aikido population. At present aikido is practiced in 140 countries and regions in the world by approximately 1,600,000 people.

It is a great contribution to world peace to have many people in the world who pursue the same art. This peace-loving aspect of aikido was highly estimated overseas, and he was awarded an honorary Ph.D from University of Valencia and had an audience with the Pope. These honours confirmed his determination to make further contributions to world peace. In Japan he was conferred a Blue Ribbon Medal in 1986 (at

Left: Kisshomaru the second Doshu who was just awarded an honorary Ph.D from University of Valencia (then the College of Engeneering) in 1992;
Right: Kisshomaru the second Doshu having an audience with Pope John Paul II in 1994

the age of sixty-five), the Third Order of the Sacred Treasure in 1995 (at the age of seventy-four).

I am determined to stay focused on the tradition he established and make further efforts to protect and develop aikido so that it can be valuable to society. Furthermore, I will try my best in my everyday lives to improve myself in order to pursue my own art of aikido.

Before I started substantial training as undergraduate student, the Hombu Dojo was, to use an indiscreet expression once again, a part of my playground. I sometimes tried an imitation of aikido training and at other times, especially in the afternoon, I played with neibourhood children only to be chided by adults. To me, live-in disciples and other students who came to dojo for training were just like members of my extended family. To look back on those days, things were really moving so slowly.

Live-in disciples before the war lived in the dojo and

Kisshomaru the second Doshu at one of the parties for celebrating his reception of a Blue Ribbon Medal in 1986, where masters, instructors, and members of the staff at the Hombu Dojo were present; the author at the right end in the first row; next to him but two Kisshomaru the second Doshu and his wife Sakuko

presumably had nothing to do other than to clean it, tidy up the garden and ground before the gate, and practice aikido. I would fold a paper airplane and fly it in the empty dojo.

Some trainees often asked me, 'Are you studying hard?' when I was an elementary school pupil and said to me, 'Hey, practice aikido' when I was a secondary-school student. To such questions and directions I just smiled but thought inside, 'It's none of your business'. Although my father told me to study, he never told me explicitly to practice aikido. I still remember feeling somewhat rebellious against those directions that came not from my parents but from outsiders.

Kisshomaru the second Doshu was decorated with the
Third Order of the Sacred Treasure in 1995

In those days everything around aikido was moving very
slowly in the run-up to its leap to the higher position where
it gained wider recognition in society. There was no Sunday
training session. In the 20s of the Showa era lessons at the
Hombu Dojo were given twice a day, one in the morning (from
six a.m.) and the other in the evening (from six p.m.), each of
which lasted about an hour. Around the 30th year of the Showa
era, three additional sessions started, respectively beginning
at eight a.m., three p.m., and five p.m. In the mid 30s of the
Showa era Sunday training started.

After all, it was my father who divided up sessions so that
each may equally end in one hour. We are so accustomed to our
present system that we find nothing odd about it, but before
the war there was no such division. The Founder demonstrated
a model technique, his disciples practiced it, the Founder

The Hombu Dojo circa the 30th year of the Showa era; to the author as a child it was my home and a playground when it was empty; students almost felt like members of my extended family.

demonstrated another technique, they practiced it again, and so on and so forth. The length of one session depended entirely on what they were practicing. Sometimes they only practiced sitting techniques for a considerable length of time. Of course, no disciple dared to ask the Founder to move on to another technique.

The Greatest Turning Point after the War

In 1956 my father left his company and decided to establish himself solely as an aikido teacher. His decision was triggered by the persuasion from one of his fellow workers. Mr. Shigeo Tokunaga—who was later to be Promotion Director of the Central League of Professional Baseball and Managing Director of the Aikikai Foundation—who was working for the Osaka Trading Company took a look at my grandfather's demonstration and said to my father who was also watching the demonstration with him: 'This is really great. Mr. Ueshiba, why are you working for our company when you have such a great job to do at home? Who else is to succeed your father in this job except you?' Then my father made up his mind to leave the company and devote himself entirely to aikido, as I was told.

As society began to settle down, disciples from the prewar period came back to training and new students started coming in. Since around the 31st year of the Showa era, those refugees who had lived in our house from the end of the war gradually left us, and, with the last family moving out to Ogikubo, the whole dojo became available for training.

Looking back on the history of aikido, I keenly realize that the greatest turning point after the war was the time when the Hombu Dojo was rebuilt and the Founder passed away. On December the 15th 1968 the three-storied (now five-storied) building of the new Hombu Dojo was completed, and the inauguration ceremony was held on January 12th the next year. On October 5th the same year 'All Japan Aikido Demonstration in Celebration of the Completion of the New Building' was held in the Hibiya Public Hall, and the Founder demonstrated his splendid art.

Now I can imagine how great pains my father took in embarking on the project of building a modern three-storied dojo of reinforced concrete, but at that time, when I was just a

The Hombu Dojo was rebuild into a new building in 1968; right: the old Hombu Dojo circa 1967, right before reconstruction; left: the present Hombu Dojo, which is now five-storied after some processes of enlargement

first-year high-school student, I missed my old beloved house so much and was so depressed at the thought of necessarily moving to live in a temporary residence until the completion of a new building that I could not see what my father was thinking inside.

With the completion of the new Hombu Dojo, live-in disciples who had lived in the old dojo became commuters. January the 15th in the next year, the Mirror Opening Ceremony was held as usual. The Founder was fine at that time, but suddenly got out of condition right after that and passed away at five a.m. on April 26 th at the age of eighty six. My father immediately became Doshu and took over the lineage of aikido. In October the 7th All Japan Aikido Demonstration was held in memory of the Founder.

The Doshu of Aikido is now to be taken over by the lineal descendant who is faithful to the Founder's ideals. When the Founder passed away in 1969, high-ranking disciples seemed

The Founder demonstrating techniques at the Mirror Opening Ceremony right after the inauguration ceremony; this was his last performance.

to be worried about whether or not my father would be able to take over the position smoothly. However, it was only a few people that disapproved of the hereditary system of succession and even founded their own schools by saying, 'I'm the Founder's disciple, not Mr. Kisshomaru's'. Almost all of the disciples believed so firmly that it would take many generations to complete one martial art and after all trusted my father so much that they approved of his succession to the position of Doshu.

As a matter of fact, after the war, it was substantially my father who arranged everything about the operation of the Hombu Dojo including the way morning sessions were organized and the management of Aikikai. Of course, the Founder's strict teachings stayed as they were. So far as aikido

The second Doshu at the succession ceremony on June 14th, 1970; Kisshomaru the second Doshu (the second from the left), Mitsujiro Ishii, the former Speaker of the House of Representatives and Director of the Aikikai Foundation (the third), Sunao Sonoda, the former Minister of Foreign Affairs and Director of the Aikikai Foundation (the fourth)

was concerned, my father never slighted the Founder. As regards the public demonstration that marked the greatest turning point of aikido in the century, my father proposed the idea over and over again, persistently gave his opinions, and tried very hard to get his approval.

Although his sharp eyes might have given him a forbidding look, my father was not an inapproachable person. He had even been a favourite with his seniors since he was young, though it might have been difficult to imagine from his look. After all, he rarely contradicted his seniors.

He also behaved modestly when he was working for his

company. He never said anything impudent on the spur of the moment but tried to persuade people logically. Directors of the company evaluated his way of reasoning and communication so much, as Mr. Hideo Yonemochi (the former Managing Director of the Aikikai Foundation) who worked under my father later told me, that they all depended on him for help whenever occasion arises. Mr. Yonemochi also told me that my father was a man of integrity.

Going Forward Together

The Ueshiba family coexists with aikido, and its head dojo with Aikikai. In close relation to them there are the All Japan Aikido Association and many other aikido-related organizations. What Morihei Ueshiba created was taken over by Kisshomaru in a direct line, and further by me who continued to practice beside Kisshomaru and worked with him in the management of the Hombu Dojo and Aikikai. Thus the lineage and organization of aikido go on naturally and without any conflicts. A hereditary system, which has been adopted by many of our traditional arts and fitted neatly into Japanese culture, is presumably one of the most excellent inventions of which Japan can be proud before the world.

Having said that, in the case of aikido, we also have to think about how techniques and training methods are taken over. One cannot be a universally acknowledged successor simply by being related to the predecessor by blood. It is not a matter of whether the successor is strong or weak or skilled in applying techniques or not. What is really expected of a successor is that the person has a long experience of training and is able to keep going forward, based on the ideals of aikido, together with all the people in the world who practice aikido.

Since aikido-related organizations are expanding and so many people are involved in them, I gradually get to understand my own function in each of the individual situations that occur. What is important is to take a broad view of things and read people's thoughts from what they say. My father told me nothing about what I should do or how I should behave as Doshu. Instead he told me to suppress likes and dislikes about people in training and to treat with equal consideration all the students who come to the dojo. I also engraved on my heart some pieces of his advice: do not contradict someone outright; keep my promise; do not betray anyone; and, after all, put myself in the other person's place.

Among the people practicing aikido at dojo, there is a great difference between those specializing in aikido and other ordinary members. The goals of training are different between aikido specialists and other people, so my father told me not to see people only from my point of view.

There are many masters in the department of instruction in the Hombu Dojo who are older than I. There used to be others who had started aikido much earlier than I and belonged to my father's generation, working with him when he was just a member of Aikikai, and I made a point of modestly listening to their opinions. An organization consists of people. It is impossible to do every little thing for oneself, and we have to collaborate with each other. The basic principle in working with people is to treat people with consideration. It is important also to set a good example, take a broad view of things, and guide

The author presiding at the Board of Directors; in addition to technical instruction, it is also one of his most important duties to take care of the operation of the whole organization as Chief Director.

members to work properly so that they can play their respective roles in the organization.

As regards technical instruction, we need to keep the basics as they are no matter how expanded the organization becomes. The more expanded it is, the more important to keep the centre solidly. Of course, it is also important to consider the general trend of the age, figure out what should or should not be changed, and make flexible decisions accordingly. As time goes by, we have to face many different problems, and I hope I can take a good look at the trend of the times and cope properly with the problems that arise from time to time.

A Member of the Ueshiba Family Should Take Charge of Training at the Hombu Dojo Once a Day

Another important rule, which the Founder made and has been handed down through my father to the following generations, is 'a member of the Ueshiba family should take charge of training at the Hombu Dojo once a day'. As a matter of fact, it is possible to ask someone to take charge of morning sessions. Yet, we have always been faithful to our principle of disciplining ourselves in taking charge of training with a strong sense of mission. Once determined to take over the tradition of aikido, Doshu should never fail to take charge of training at his dojo. This is the way we practice what we preach.

You cannot motivate your students to practice aikido just by ordering them to do so. Instead, we go to morning sessions ourselves. I believe that aikido today is based on our persistent efforts to take the lead in everyday training. In so doing, after all, we are putting into practice the principle the Founder established of prioritizing daily training. As aikido becomes more popularized, we need to take care of an increasingly wider variety of jobs concerning the management of the organization of Aikikai. Still, once we prioritize those jobs and stop going to dojo, aikido will lose its centre.

In aikido the basic principle is 'training first'. If instructors are all talk and no action, students will not follow them. They need to move together with students and show them how techniques work. My father was well aware of the function of

The author who never fails to take charge of training at the Hombu Dojo as long as he is in Tokyo

an instructor. Some people might have said to him, 'Considering your age, you don't have to take charge of training at dojo', but he would never have listened to such advice. I am proudly aware of the importance of the incumbent Doshu taking charge of training at the Hombu Dojo, that is, the Ueshiba Dojo; for only by practicing what he preaches, he can convincingly bring the whole organization together. Only by fixing the centre, you can make everything around it stable. This is true of any organization.

What It Means for a Direct Descendent to Take over the Tradition of Aikido

The Ueshiba family coexists with aikido, and its head dojo with Aikikai. This premise may need further elaboration to be understood by members of Aikikai. For if its central principle gets unstable, aikido will dwindle to a vanishing point.

There is a world of difference between those people whose parents work away from home, for example, as company employees and others born and bred in close relationship with their respective family businesses and exposed from childhood to all the information concerning them, regardless of which group is more blessed of the two. My son Mitsuteru, now Director of the Head Dojo, and I belong to the latter group. We have both taken over the mission of the head family of aikido. I sometimes think that we are very much like families that are engaged in domestic handicraft industry.

If we accept the circumstances as they are, without considering them unfortunate, and go on living with them, good results will surely arise. Having said that, we all have special feelings about the circumstances we were born into, and I would be lying if I said I found nothing unsatisfactory about my lot.

My circumstances may look much more grave than they really are if I describe them with such expressions as 'resolution', 'responsibility', and 'a sense of mission'. What really happened was that I was born into the Ueshiba family, found a dojo of aikido close by, and grew up with aikido, which was almost

The author as *uke* to his father, Kisshomaru the second Doshu, at All Mitsubishi Budo Demonstration in 1974

a part of my everyday life. I always saw my father teaching classes every day and vaguely thought, around the time when I was a high-school student, that I would step into his shoes in due course of time. I also attended his lessons before I came into a leading position, and in the natural course of events I am now taking charge of training every morning.

Parents and children are also human individuals with different opinions, which may sometimes clash with each other. However, it is not the case with us, because in our family a son never contradicts his father. It is not because we are an excellent family but presumably because we have lived in an environment in which such a father-son relationship is perfectly familiar to us.

The author giving a model demonstration with his son Mitsuteru (Director of the Head Dojo) as *uke* at All Japan Aikido Demonstration

Promotion of aikido overseas started when live-in disciples were sent one by one to foreign countries, and aikido is now practiced widely even in developing countries. As the organization expands, an increasing number and variety of problems arise. We have to be flexible in handling them lest we should get entangled in further complications. In order to be able to do so, we need discernment in judging things. I am now planning to do what I can do for the next several years, expecting the next generation to learn something from me and take care of the rest in their own ways.

What is more and more important in coming years is our ability to put people together. In order to hold the ability, we need to keep the tradition of aikido stable. I also think it

The author with his first son Mitsuteru at All Japan Aikido Demonstration

important that the Hombu Dojo, that is the Ueshiba Dojo, which is the centre of the whole organization, should also be the place where everyday training is properly going on and send out to the world such good messages as can constitute the leading principles of aikido. As times change, people's ways of thinking change. We cannot ignore the influence of the trend of the times. As times change, some people may leave us. It is a sad thing, but we cannot stop them if they do so in the natural course of events. It is more important to properly keep doing what we should do rather than to try to take care of such a negative phenomenon. As long as we are faithful to the Founder's ideals, I believe that good results will naturally come out.

My son Mitsuteru was born into the same circumstances as mine, started his career at Aikikai as a member of its staff, and now serves as Director of the Hombu Dojo. The direct descendants of the Founder have steadily following the Way, and I hope it is greatly reassuring to aikido students to see the tradition properly carried on and find themselves deeply connected to the Founder's genuine art of aikido.

What looks odd or eccentric right before your eyes does not last long, no matter how striking it is. What is important is to carefully practice aikido that was handed down from the Founder to Kisshomaru the second Doshu and then to pass it down to the next generation in its genuine style. I think it is my duty and the duty of the Doshu of the time who keeps the tradition alive. The tradition of aikido has come down to us along the direct line of the head family. This is the way the tradition is taken over by direct descendants.

Culture in Dojo

When you apply a grappling technique, you finally pin your opponent down in the sitting posture. We also have sitting techniques and half-sitting-half-standing techniques that you apply in the sitting posture with your knees on the mat. The posture is familiar to Japanese people, but there are many countries in which people do not sit on the floor, and therefore we need to teach them how to sit in the formal *seiza* posture and how to make a bow in it. There are an increasing number of houses without any straw-mat room even in Japan, and Japanese people do not sit in the *seiza* posture as often as they used to, much less roll on a tatami. Nevertheless, if we stop practicing grappling techniques, sitting or half-sitting-half-

The author teaching a training session for instructors
sponsored by the Aikikai Public Utility Foundation

sanding techniques, what we practice is not aikido any more.

When I succeeded to the position of Doshu, I did not think of starting anything new and original. All I was planning to do was to take over my father's project of making the Founder's art of aikido accessible to the general public and make partial changes needed to make it suit the times. One of the things I actually did was, for example, to develop the network of leagues in all the prefectures in Japan to strengthen the cooperative relationship between the Hombu Dojo and affiliated dojos in consideration of the expansion of the whole organization. In so doing, I also systematized the way we can activate training sessions as well as trainer-training sessions in each prefecture and further respond quickly to the request for instructors from junior-high schools that adopt aikido as one of the elective subjects in their budo curriculum.

Another thing, if it is worth mentioning, is the quakeproofing of the Hombu Dojo. Since the present dojo was built in 1968, I decided to have it examined by the present quakeproofing standards and accordingly reinforced so that it might not to be destroyed even by such a great earthquake as matches the Great Hanshin and Awaji Earthquake. I also made sure that automatic external defibrillators should be placed properly. It is important to make changes in the organization and facilities to meet the needs of the times.

On the other hand, we should not change the essential parts of aikido. Take the cleaning of the Hombu Dojo for example. At present, its main entrance, corridors, and toilets are cleaned by the instructors on night duty, but the training rooms are cleaned by our students at the end of their training. Big cleanups that are held at every turn of the seasons every year are taken care of mainly by the managers of the Hombu Dojo and its students. It is possible to hire professional cleaners, but I would rather not do so, because I firmly believe that it is important for students to become attached to their 'own' dojo, willing to clean the place where they train themselves, and grateful to the place itself; that dojo relies for healthy operation on its students' positive emotional involvement in it.

On the occasions of annual All Japan Aikido Demonstration, Hombu Dojo trainees help us greatly behind the scenes, which is also the case on many other occasions including Mirror Opening Day in January. Years ago university aikido clubs provided us with an adequate number of helping hands, but as the annual demonstration meeting gets more large-scale, we need more hands outside university clubs. I am really grateful to those Hombu Dojo trainees.

The author talking joyfully at the party after All Japan Aikido Demonstration with Hombu Dojo trainees and university students who helped its operation behind the scenes

When my father was at the position of Doshu, Hombu Dojo trainees already organized many social gatherings, and their attachment for the Hombu Dojo and the tradition of their voluntary engagement in its operation seem to be taken over by its present members in many different forms. Twenty years have already passed since Oshin-kai was established as one of my friendship societies. We have annual mid-summer and year-end parties with members of those societies, and I like to talk to trainees and make a point of attending them whenever time permits.

The Hombu Dojo is the core of Aikikai and at the same time the first dojo the Founder established himself. This may be one of the reasons why its regular members especially have a strong sense of unity. Many people come to the Hombu Dojo from far away by car, but we do not have a big parking lot. Therefore, some of them, who are attending the first morning session from six thirty, park their cars in the parking areas nearby before six o'clock and wait in their cars for the Dojo to open at six. I am always impressed with their enthusiasm.

What we experience at dojo is not just technical developments or enjoyment of training. With its own culture dojo is more than just a physical training facility. It is a place where many people, children and old people alike, interact with each other, train each other, develop vital force, and enrich their own lives without any consideration about title, sex, age, or even nationality. What we enjoy at the dojo of aikido is presumably a culture of which Japan can be proud before the whole world.

There are many more important things in moving things forward than rationalization and modernization, and I think this is also true of any field of human activities. Some groups or organizations seem to make drastic changes in their policies right after their heads change, but I never thought of making the same thing happen to our organization. I will keep what should not be changed as it is and let natural changes take place.

The Hombu Dojo of Aikido

When I am in Tokyo, I make a point of going to dojo to take charge of the first morning session of the day and practice with my students. I really wish I could go to all the classes conducted in the Hombu Dojo every day, but there are so many students and classes, and on top of that I have so many local training sessions and annual meetings to attend that unfortunately I cannot take care of everything.

Fortunately, however, we have masters in the Hombu Dojo who have long experiences of proper training. At present, qualification for conducting promotion examinations is given to high-rankers from six dan upwards, and we make a distinction between those high-rankers and others below six dan by calling the former 'masters' and the latter 'instructors'. It is possible, of course, for someone below six dan to open a dojo of aikido, but he or she needs to ask for the presence of a master from six dan upwards to conduct a promotion test.

Many people ask me what is the difference between the masters of the Hombu Dojo and those of affiliated dojos. The masters of Hombu Dojo are all professional aikidoists unlike most of the other masters, spend more time practicing aikido than the others, and most importantly keep on training at the Hombu Dojo of Aikido which is the very centre of the Aikikai Public Utility Foundation under the tutelage of the Doshu of the time who is a direct descendant of the Ueshibas from the Founder of aikido through Kisshomaru the second Doshu and me. The Hombu Dojo masters therefore have taken over the most fundamental techniques of aikido.

I frequently tell our masters and instructors at the Hombu Dojo that Hombu Dojo aikidoists should be proud of practicing aikido which has been directly handed down in the Ueshiba family but, more importantly, that they should be modest enough to always examine their own skills. I strongly believe that we should make our own efforts before expecting members of our registered dojos to support the whole organization of aikido. It is impossible, of course, for the Hombu Dojo masters to teach their classes exactly the same way. They all differ from each other in physical constructions and movements.

The author giving a speech at the party celebrating the eightieth anniversary of the Hombu Dojo and seventieth anniversary of Aikikai

Nevertheless, we are trying our best every day to keep the general framework of genuine and high-quality techniques at the Hombu Dojo so that they may not deviate from the basics.

Another question which some people seriously ask me is whether there are any special techniques which have been handed down secretly only in the Ueshiba family over four generations from the Founder through Kisshomaru the second Doshu to me and further to Mitsuteru the Director of the Head Dojo. Indeed, if you keep on with your daily training for a long time, you will get a glimpse of something very special—something that is sometimes referred to as the 'Way'. My father did not learn aikido under the Founder's attentive supervision, nor did Mitsuteru and I receive any detailed technical instruction from our predecessors. What Mitsuteru did was simply to attend Kisshomaru the second Doshu's lessons and feel the general atmosphere of training.

If there can be anything special that has been passed down in the Ueshiba family, it would be the Hombu Dojo itself. This is the dojo—originally the Kobukan Ueshiba Dojo established in the same place—where the art of aikido, which the Founder completed after years of assiduous effort and study, has been developed and passed down to its trainees up to the present.

If you simply want to learn aikido techniques, it is not very difficult today with so many dojos around—astonishing in number in contrast to those in the postwar period in the 20s and 30s of Showa—and so many different and convenient learning methods including the use of videos and DVDs. Nevertheless, we have no end of aikido students every year, inside and outside Japan, who come all the way to the Hombu Dojo to join our training. I am really glad to hear them say that they want to train in the Hombu Dojo in Tokyo, Japan, just once in a lifetime. If they cannot afford to do so, they say, at least they want to have a master from the Hombu Dojo at their special training or trainer-training sessions. We now have an increasing number of requests for travelling Hombu Dojo instructors every year.

If the secrets or esoterics of aikido are condensed in its basics, the Hombu Dojo indeed is most faithful to the very basics. Moreover, in order to make as many aikido students learn them, we are increasing the number of travelling instructors who supervise training sessions overseas. We also established mutually cooperative aikido associations in all the prefectures in Japan in 2012 as well as the system for sending Hombu Dojo instructors to supervise the training and trainer-training sessions sponsored by those associations.

I am happy to have many people seeking a job as an instructor at the Hombu Dojo, but I am afraid to say that the job is not as easy as they think. You cannot become an aikido instructor simply because you like aikido or want to practice it every day. The greatest problem is whether or not you have a mentality suitable to become one. Apart from the question of whether the candidate is physically talented or not, once employed as an instructor, he or she has to keep practicing aikido every day. It may be enjoyable at first, but before long training as part of your job can sometimes get trying. What I know very well myself, working for Aikikai, is that it is difficult for someone to continue aikido only as an instructor unless he or she can take a positive attitude towards training.

One possible way to see how suited you are for an aikido instructor is to think about how you spend the New Year or summer holidays, which are longer at the Hombu Dojo than at ordinary companies. On the first day of the holidays, your body will be aching all over, but after a couple of days you may be itching to practice aikido. Furthermore, on the fourth day, you may feel your body getting stiff and want to train as soon as possible. If this is what you feel, you will be suited for an instructor.

Resolution

The first aikido demonstration meeting I participated in was the fourth general demonstration meeting held at the Hibiya Public Hall in 1964. Since there was no children's class in the Hombu Dojo in those days—it was in 1974 that children's classes were set up—and I participated in the meeting as a member of the 'voluntary groups of children from the Hombu Dojo of Aikido'. I went onto the stage with five groups of junior-high-school students who were my seniors by one year. I do not remember the techniques we performed in detail, but if I remember rightly, I was not very nervous before a great number of spectators.

After the demonstration there was a party for everybody involved, but we children did not take part in it. My father brought us back home by taxi and gave us sweets he had bought. After that he went back to the venue of the party.

Although I was practicing aikido since childhood, I never thought of following in my father's footsteps as a child; I was not forced to take lessons on a daily basis, and after all I had an elder brother. My brother was also practicing aikido in the same way but stopped practicing when he entered university to concentrate on his undergraduate study. That was the time when I thought for the first time, 'If my brother isn't going to take over the job, I'll have to'. It was when I was a high-school student.

After entering university, I started my training on a regular basis, and after a couple of years I sometimes joined my father's classes as *uke* to him when he could find no instructor available. When my father went to Europe at the invitation of Aikikai in European countries in 1975, he brought me with him and introduced me everywhere as his son, thereby making many people tacitly assume that I would be his successor and reminding me of my duty to take over the tradition of aikido.

I never expressed my resolution to take over the lineage to my father, who on his part never told me to do so. I simply made a suggestion in our casual conversation at home that I would help him with the job of the Doshu, to which he simply made a brief approval by saying, 'Oh, that's good'. Without confirming my intention by words, my father seemed to have a tacit understanding that I would succeed him. He was not the type of a person who would put into words what he thought. Nor did he give me any minute directions even concerning aikido training. All he said was 'Keep training, and you will naturally get a good grasp of technical details'.

How I Started Teaching

Since I entered university, substantial training started for me. I began by serving as *uke* in Kisshomaru the second Doshu's morning classes. I also took charge of women's classes when we did not have enough instructors available. When I first declined to teach those classes by saying, 'I'm still a student, and I don't think I can do it', Master Kisaburo Osawa, the then Director of the Hombu Dojo, responded, 'Are you fully aware what kind of dojo this is? This is the Ueshiba Dojo. Who else will take care of it, if you don't?' and persuaded me into teaching a women's class. I asked some of the ladies I had known from morning classes to join it so that I might get less nervous, and I managed to do my first job as an instructor.

Right after I graduated from university and started working for Aikikai, I first took charge of individual tutoring. About three months later, one of the masters became indisposed and unable to teach classes, and I had to fill up the vacancy and take charge of beginner's classes. This is how I started substantial teaching. Then, I took charge of intermediate classes in the Aikido Academy and later beginner's morning classes on Monday, Wednesday, and Friday.

What I found really challenging when I started teaching beginner's classes was to teach those students who had had no experience of training. As someone who was brought up in the circumstances where aikido was part of daily lives, I had no experience of learning aikido as a beginner. All I had done was to see people practice techniques and naturally learn them, and I had never been taught them systematically.

After warming up and exercises of basic movements I demonstrated model techniques and invited my students to do the same, but beginners would have been quite at a loss what to do. Partly because they were nervous, they moved their arms and feet in a totally confused manner. I had some difficulty understanding why they moved the way they did. Then I read my father's books on aikido techniques so that I could explain them systematically in words and make them understood by any student. It was a very good opportunity to realize the importance of theorizing anew what I had learned physically.

It would be unthinkable in an ordinary situation that an inexperienced instructor should teach beginner's classes, but

The author watching his students training enthusiastically

in retrospect I might have been expected, as Ueshiba's son and heir, to go through on-the-job training of aikido instruction. Now I am much better at teaching beginners, and when I teach university students, for example, I pay attention to what their personalities are and how nervous they are. I am following my father's teachings that we need to put ourselves in the place of other people and that we need to observe other people carefully.

Trainees differ from each other in terms of age, experiences, physical construction and features. Some learn very quickly, and others slowly. You cannot teach all of them in exactly the same way. They all differ in character as well. Some like to teach other students, others just practice as they are told. There are also those who have strong characters. It is also important to pay attention to the combination of *uke* and *tori*. Another important thing is that instructors should not impose on their students what they have acquired through long years of strenuous training but watch over and guide them carefully.

Each instructor needs to take care of about fifty students in one class and, therefore, cannot teach individual students closely. What instructors need to do instead is, first of all, to demonstrate the whole flow of movements—application of *kokyu-ryoku*, unbalancing, throwing, pinning, and so on—and then, without trying to teach individual students closely, aim at the collective development of techniques, moving together with their students and giving them proper pieces of advice.

I make a point of advising our instructors to learn how to handle teaching situations while practicing aikido with their students or fellow trainees. It sometimes happens, especially with young instructors, that students have longer experiences of training. In such a case, I advise them to respect those senior students for their rich social experiences and try to learn from them.

My father often told me, when we went to training sessions or demonstration meetings, what I would need to mind on those occasions: 'Look around the place and try to grasp how many people there are, what kind of people they are, and what is the general atmosphere of the whole event.' It is the duty of someone in charge of an event or in the position of an instructor to grasp those things instantly in order to organize the event smoothly. On the occasion when many people get together in one place, anything might happen at any moment. By putting ourselves in the place of others, taking a good look at them and a broad view over things, as my father's advice goes, we can make ourselves imperturbable at any unexpected

The author giving a closing statement at the end of All Japan Aikido Demonstration as sponsor and chairman of the meeting

accident. My father's advice is based on his deep involvement in martial arts from the prewar period.

Let me digress here briefly to talk about what happened right after I started working for Aikikai as an instructor. At the beginning of your career as an instructor you had to (and still have to) live in the Hombu Dojo. The second office in the present Hombu Dojo used to be something like a lumber room, where live-in instructors and I, all close in age, sometimes got together to have a secret drinking session. At first we were drinking rather quietly, but once our trainees finished changing clothes and left the dojo, we got more drunk and boisterous with our peals of laughter carrying outside. Unfortunately, we had the Ueshibas' house next door. When my father was hale and hearty, being a heavy drinker himself, he just laughed away our merrymaking, but my mother responded rather differently. 'You are still drinking! It's time to stop it!' She often snapped at us and made us clear out.

As long as I was following the basic moral principles—keeping promises, observing rules, taking responsibilities, not troubling others, and so on—I was never scolded by my father even for going on a binge. I would have been, of course, if I had missed a morning training session owing to a hangover. Otherwise, my father was not a nagging parent. He often went for a drink himself with his disciples, but no matter how late he came back, he never failed to teach a session the next morning. He hardly smiled in the presence of other people and might have looked intimidating to someone who did not know him, but as a matter of fact he was a placid, generous and big-hearted person.

Strength and Generosity Acquired Through Hardships

When Japanese society was still going through hard times, my predecessors kept aikido alive, firmly believing, 'We can do it; we must do it'. Then, their disciples went overseas to teach and promote aikido, thereby expanding its sphere to the world. The struggle to keep aikido alive had already started in the Founder's days. Yoroku, the Founder's father, sold his fields in Kishu piece by piece to support his son financially until his son created the art of aikido. When the war broke out, the Founder, without any means to gain an income, went to Iwama to provide for himself and kept aikido alive. During the war, my father remained in Tokyo and saved the Hombu Dojo till the end. When a fire broke out in the dojo, neighbours were so impressed to see my father trying desperately to bring it under control alone that they formed a bucket brigade and helped him extinguish it.

Having already spent most of the Ueshibas' wealth, my father had to struggle through financial difficulties from the 20s of the Showa era, right before the high economic growth started, to the 30s, when he was not yet sure whether or not he could make a living. His generosity and big-heartedness might have been based on his experiences of struggling through those hard times. Right after the war, my father took care of the dojo, while earning his living as a company employee. It was also the time when aikido enthusiasts began to come to the Hombu Dojo with nothing and virtually 'lived in' the dojo to practice aikido; when nobody knew what would happen to it.

Some masters reminisced about how my father responded to those live-in disciples who could not afford to pay tuition fees: he simply said 'That's fine' to them and never demanded the payment. He sometimes gave them his pocket money and prepared meals for them, while dining with his family. It is not very difficult to imagine what my mother had to go through to support him. My mother rarely commented on aikido and live-in disciples but looked really relieved when, with the new dojo completed in the 1968, the house of the Ueshiba family was separated from the Hombu Dojo.

Until then I had found it quite natural to live with many other people as with members of my extended family. There were aikido-related people as well as war refugees living in one part of the dojo. Day trainees were only seven or eight a day, some of whom took a shower in our family bathroom, poured water over themselves at the well, or washed their training wear by stamping on it at the bathroom. The old Ueshiba Dojo was really like a big comfortable house of a large family. We took meals separately depending on how we were respectively engaged on the day—training, working outside, going to school, and so on—but we all 'ate from the same pot', as a Japanese idiom goes, under the same roof. The meals in those days were much more homely than what we eat today, but they still remain in me as a fond memory accompanied by the sound of joyful voices of many people.

My father made a decision to be a full-time aikidoist in 1956, which, in retrospect, seems to be extremely well timed. If he had made the decision in the 20s of the Showa era, we would have gone through far more serious financial difficulties and might possibly have had to place our head dojo not in Tokyo but in Iwama and reduce the whole organization considerably. On the other hand, if my father had worked for his company for much longer, the promotion of aikido in Japan and overseas would have been delayed by ten years or more.

In my impression my father had always been well taken care of as the only son of the Founder. He was taken to formal gatherings and, on many occasions, photographed together with the Founder. It was not the case with me. I was a second son, after all, and did not appear formally in the presence of many people. That well-bred father underwent great hardships after the war. Throughout the turbulent period he kept aikido alive, and thanks to his strenuous efforts we have Aikikai today. I do not want all its ordinary members to know its history but really hope that the masters and instructors in Aikikai and

The Founder and Kisshomaru the second Doshu talking joyfully with their disciples at the old Hombu Dojo circa 1956

professional aikidoists at least should know what my father went through.

Many trainees at the Hombu Dojo of Aikido today may think that there used to be a similar dojo in this place with the Founder supervising training sessions every morning. In reality, all we had was one morning session and one evening session every day with seven or eight students. Nothing else. There were also some people who came to the dojo because they had no other place to stay. Aikido was practiced under totally different circumstances from what we know today.

In the beginning aikido was born, and in order to keep it alive our predecessors established an organization called Aikikai, which has developed into our Public Utility Foundation. At the same time we have established aikido associations in all the prefectures and tried to solidify their networks. Everyone has his or her role to play. A serious disaster may happen at any moment if we misunderstand our own roles. Never forget the ideals you entertained in the beginning. Of course, I am always telling this to myself.

My Greatest Ordeal

I was born into the Ueshiba family and have practiced aikido for a long time, and naturally the meetings of All Japan Aikido Demonstration I attended are all impressed in my memory, but the most memorable meeting was the 17th All Japan Aikido Demonstration in 1979. This is how it impressed itself so deeply in my memory:

On April 14th the same year my father went to Ginza to make a new suit, bringing me with him. On our return home, he suddenly said, 'I have stomach ache'.

'Let's buy a stomach medicine in Shinjuku and go home,' I said. We took a taxi and went for a while, when he again said, 'I have stomach ache'. He was normally a very patient person, and this was something very unusual for him to say. On arriving home, he crouched down at the gate and stayed there motionless.

We immediately called for our family doctor, who, seeing his abdomen swollen, said, 'Call for an ambulance quickly, because this is beyond my capacity of treatment'. We did as we were told, and my father was taken by ambulance to Tokyo Women's Medical University Hospital.

It was Saturday, unfortunately, and there was no doctor in charge. My wife was quick-witted enough to visit Mr. Morimasa Yoshioka (later President of Tokyo Women's Medical University) in the neighbourhood to ask him to arrange that my father should be admitted to the hospital.

The next day, an abdominal section was performed on my father to pinpoint the cause of his stomachache, which turned out to be a twisted intestine. The cause having been identified, a further operation was performed to remove three fourths of his small intestine, and he had to stay in hospital until early July. He was aged fifty-eight at that time. Until that time he had never got drunk in the presence of other people; he even was a heavy drinker when young. However, after this time, intoxication began to reveal itself on his face when he drank with other people, suggesting that he became unable to drink as much as he used to.

One of the things we did right after he was hospitalized was to bring a whiteboard into his sickroom and copied on it everything that was written on his datebook. We discussed his schedule and decided how to deal with what he had been planning to do one by one. Although I was still twenty-eight at that time, I immediately took office as one of the directors of Aikikai just in case any unexpected misfortune might take place. Concerning the management of training at the dojo and the operation of Aikikai and its offices, I had no apprehension because we had Master Kisaburo Osawa, then Director of the Hombu Dojo, and other experienced masters and instructors, and able members of the staff.

My greatest worry concerned All Japan Aikido Demonstration, the greatest annual event of Aikikai, which was to be held in

May. It was (and still is) the incumbent Doshu's duty to give a 'general demonstration' at the end of the meeting, and with my father still in bed, I had to perform the duty. I had taken part in the annual meetings with other masters in 1977 and 78 but had never been the last and most important performer at the event. It was the third year since we moved the venue of the event to the Nippon Budokan, and the participants and spectators, far fewer than we have every year today, barely filled the seats on the first floor. I was already the Assistant Director of the Hombu Dojo on one hand but on the other just a 'stripling' who had been training with other instructors of the same generation and having drinking bouts with them. I as well as the Ueshibas would have to take the heavy responsibility: I for giving the last demonstration at All Japan Aikido Demonstration in place of the then Dohsu, the Ueshibas for allowing this to happen.

I guess that people around me were also worried. Would it not be better to ask one of the high-rank masters or Master Kisaburo Osawa, Director of the Hombu Dojo, to do the job, or would there be another choice? Master Kisaburo Osawa's words were decisive: 'The person who can be the last performer in place of Kisshomaru Doshu needs to be a Hombu Dojo trainer who belongs to the Ueshiba family, that is, no other person than Moriteru-san.'

The day of All Japan Aikido Demonstration was approaching very fast, and I had no time to make mental preparation. All the eyes of five thousand people in that huge Nippon Budokan would be focused on me. Then I thought of my father who was lying in bed in Tokyo Women's Medical University Hospital.

Many people asked me later about how I practiced for the demonstration meeting, assuming that I must have made an extremely careful preparation, but what really happened was that I practiced the techniques I was to demonstrate at the meeting only once with *uke*; I did nothing else in particular. What I was expected to do technically at the meeting was to do what I had been doing in everyday instruction; the hardest part of the preparation was getting myself mentally ready for the big event.

I had already been *uke* to my father in his 'general demonstration' at the previous meetings of All Japan Aikido Demonstration, and even in preparation for my *uke* performance I had gone so far as to abstain from drinking for a month. I could not sleep well the day before each event. Yet, my tension this time was far greater than what I had felt before.

The Founder had passed away only ten years before in 1969. Many of the disciples who were with us had been initially attracted to the Founder's charisma, and there were also other aikido-related groups established by the Founder's disciples who had left us. Aikikai was not as solid as it is today. Then, my father collapsed. He lingered on the verge of death until April and just came out of the intensive care unit of the hospital in May. I was full of anxieties and could not rid myself of them easily. I was also worried about the future of Aikikai. What would happen to us, I thought. Any way, if I had to take the place of my father, I would do it properly.

I can still hear the voice of Mr. Sho Ozaki (now the Chief Director of the All Japan Aikido Association), who at that time was the master of ceremonies at the general meeting, 'Let me announce you that here comes in Mr. Moriteru Ueshiba, Assistant Director of the Hombu Dojo and Doshu-to-be', followed by a storm of applause. I have never experienced a

五つの舞台で、こもごも演武

日刊スポーツ

植芝守央氏の自由演武

The author as the final performer at All Japan Aikido
Demonstration as reported by the June 10, 1979, issue of
Aikido Newsletter

greater tension than that time in my entire life. I performed
wholeheartedly, and when I finished my demonstration, I was
extremely happy to hear another storm of applause. Older
masters also praised me by saying, 'You did a very good job'.

Extremely relieved to have carried out my duty as my father's
substitute, I went to the hospital to tell my father how the
general meeting had gone. He responded to me simply by
saying, 'Good'.

Lying in bed, my father seemed to have thought seriously
about how he would be restored to his normal state. He
resumed his instruction from the next spring and was able
to lead a normal life. I went through on-the-job training not

Kisshomaru the second Doshu heading towards the centre of the floor to give his general lecture demonstration at the end of the 35th All Japan Aikido Demonstration in 1997; This turned out to be his last demonstration in his life.

only as an aikido instructor but also as a manager of the whole organization while helping my father with his jobs. For the next twenty years he carried out his duties as our chief executive. In 1997 he became indisposed and was admitted to the Center Hospital of the National Center for Global Health and Medicine to receive a thorough workup. In the meantime I had taken office as the Director of the Hombu Dojo and Chief Director of Aikikai and gradually taken over the substantial management of the whole organization.

When the doctor in charge of my father said to me, three years before his death, 'He may pass away at any moment', I became keenly aware of my duties and formed a general plan

The author giving the closing demonstration at the 37th All Japan Aikido Demonstration which was held in 1999 'in memory of the late Kisshomaru Ueshiba Doshu'

concerning how I should manage the organization. I anticipated with resignation that some people might leave us as some of the Founder's disciples did when he passed away, but fortunately the same thing did not happen again after my father's death.

At the 37th All Japan Aikido Demonstration, which was also the meeting held in my father's memory, I was very nervous again and strongly conscious of the way I was expected to behave as Doshu. Nevertheless, I had had enough time to prepare myself mentally before the meeting, and therefore I was under less pressure in giving the final demonstration than at the 17th meeting.

This I guess was also what my father had gone through. One of my father's friends from school days once told me about how my father had felt in giving his first demonstration as Doshu in the presence of a great number of people:

'I was so impressed how you became able so soon to perform before that huge audience', his friend said to my father.

'Oh, that's because of my position,' my father replied. 'My position obliges me to do that.'

Succession to the Position of Doshu

Once having collapsed, my father never really restored his health in his later years even during the period in which his condition seemed to show a change for the better. It was largely because of his age. The doctor suggested that we should always prepare for the worst.

While keeping his true condition secret from other people than my family — as my father told us himself — I kept on with my on-the-job training as an apprentice manager of the organization so that every aikido-related activity could go on as usual. I never felt that I was working behind the scenes. I took for granted that I should respect and obey my father who was also Doshu as well as a master to me. It was also highly natural for our family to do our best to take care of the dojo, which after all was the Ueshiba Dojo.

My family seemed to be deeply concerned at that time that I might be overstressed, but I was perfectly fine; fortunately, I was not born a worrywart. In addition, having grown up in a large household, I like communicating with people, and even when I have something to worry about, I find my spirits rising while talking with other people and my anxieties gone after working up a good sweat at a morning session. A piece of advice about our health goes, 'Stress should be kept out, not in', but

I believe that it will naturally disappear while you spend your days with smiles.

In the summer of 1997 he became indisposed and was admitted to the Center Hospital of the National Center for Global Health and Medicine. The result of a workup showed abnormalities in the lungs, and the doctor in charge told us, 'If this condition goes through a normal process, I'm afraid to say he will have only a year to live. He will reach the crisis at the beginning of the New Year.' We told my father nothing about the remainder of his life.

After this, my father spent some time at home and was hospitalized again in November the same year in order to maintain his physical condition as well as to take some rest. He left the hospital at the beginning of December but discharged blood from the bowels towards the end of the year and was hospitalized again from December 28th to mid-February in 1998. This time the condition of his lungs had not worsened as apprehended, but the melena could not be taken lightly. In late March he was hospitalized for the fourth time with injured ribs, was discharged in mid-May and gave us warm words of encouragement at All Japan Aikido Demonstration. After that, he stayed at home again, taking a rest but at the same time carrying out many events with a strong sense of responsibility.

On the early morning of October 28th, with just a month to go before the end of 1998, he lapsed into a heart failure owing to the deterioration of his lung function and was suddenly hospitalized again in the Center Hospital of the National Center for Global Health and Medicine. This time his critical condition lasted as long as a week, but he made a miraculous recovery by sheer force of will and became able to speak. However, he began to deteriorate quickly around December 20th, was unable to eat anything on 23rd, and fell into critical condition again on 26th. After that he never recovered consciousness till he passed away, with our family at his deathbed, at five thirty-nine in the afternoon on January 4th in 1999.

The cause of my father's illness seemed to be a twisted intestine he had had twenty years before. It is highly likely that, since three fourths of his small intestine was removed, he could not absorb nourishment efficiently and suffered from the deterioration of lung function. Be that as it may, I was amazed at his heart function and willpower—he even asked the doctor, 'Isn't it possible to lose both lungs and still live with spirit?'—which enabled him to recover from critical conditions more than a couple of times; he really had a superhuman vitality. In addition, it seemed to me that my father, who had always been concerned about people around him, braced up his spirits to stay alive for the first three days of the New Year not to trouble people during the holidays and chose January 4th as the day for his farewell to life.

It was really trying to take care of him and keep encouraging him for a year and a half, while knowing that his days were numbered. If there had been some hope of his convalescence, if not complete recovery, my father and our family should have endured any hardship and tried our best to make it possible. However, without any hope, all our painful efforts and the treatment itself seemed to be of no avail. It was so heartbreaking to see my father taking for granted that he would be able to leave the hospital at the end of the year and getting discouraged when he deteriorated and could not eat anything. He looked really pitiful on his deathbed but at the same time

The author taking over the position of Doshu on January 18th in 1999 and Mr. Toshiki Kaifu, former Prime Minister, (now Director of the Aikikai Foundation), delivering a congratulatory address at the party held in celebration of the author's succession to Doshu at the Keio Plaza Hotel on September 25th in the same year

extremely brave after struggling with illness by willpower.

I succeeded to the position of Doshu at the age of forty-seven, which, by a curious coincidence, was the same age at which my father had taken over the lineage of aikido from the Founder. Under my father's leadership both aikido and Aikikai made a remarkable progress. Now it is my turn as Doshu, who is at the centre of all the aikido trainees in the world, to take on the heavy responsibility to further develop the already globalized art of aikido. On the other hand, I took over official duties rather smoothly and calmly thanks to my father's careful consideration about their gradual transfer.

The most important thing is, as my father always told me and as I also firmly believe, to keep supervising training sessions at

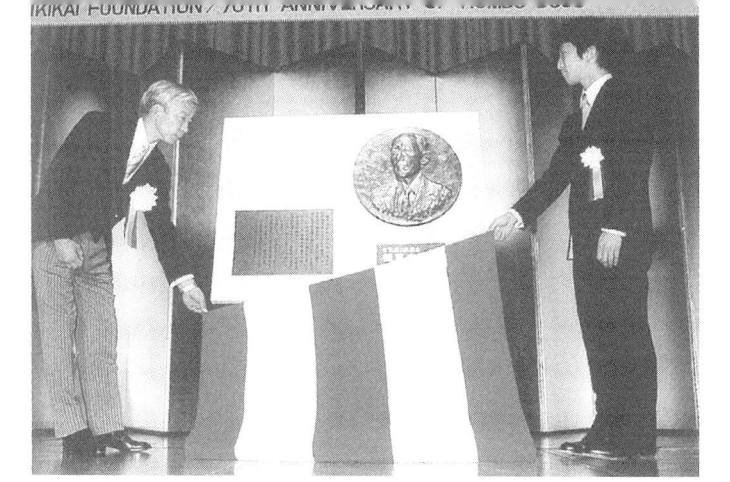

Kisshomaru the second Doshu's bust on low relief was first displayed at the party held in 2001 in celebration of the 70th anniversary of the Hombu Dojo and the 60th anniversary of the Aikikai Foundation; this relief is now displayed in the Hombu Dojo of Aikido

the Hombu Dojo. The same duties await my son Mitsuteru, the incumbent Director of the Hombu Dojo. At the age of thirty-seven he is now more heavily loaded with official duties than I was at the same age. He was playing at the dojo when he was a kindergartener and was already practicing aikido every day when he was in elementary school. I sometimes took him to demonstration meetings and training sessions inside and outside Japan. When he said to my father in hospital, 'I will take over aikido', my father beamed with joy; I still cannot forget the expression on his face.

The author together with Kisshomaru the second Doshu and Mitsuteru (now the Director of the Hombu Dojo) at the Grand Festival of the Aiki Shrine

Practicing '*Wa*'

I basically find it fairly natural that things change as times change. What is not needed in the age has to go. It is the natural course of culture, and martial arts are not exempt from it. Martial skills, which were nothing other than skills in fighting in the Warring States era, took on special spirituality under the influence of Zen Buddhism and occupied a unique position in Japanese culture as budo and, after the Meiji Restoration, played an important role in moral and physical education in school and the army. After the defeat in the Second World War, however, budo was seen in an unfavourable light and, as many people know, had to find a means of survival under the name of

The author attending the ceremony for the reception of a
Blue Ribbon Medal, which was awarded to him in 2013
for his achievements in promoting aikido

The author delivering a
speech at the general
demonstration at All Japan
Aikido Demonstration

植芝守央合気道道主藍綬褒章受章祝賀会

The author and his wife, Kyoko, looking at Mitsuteru Ueshiba, Director of the Hombu Dojo, who is delivering a closing address as the head of the organizing committee of the party held in 2014 in celebration of the author's reception of a Blue Ribbon Medal

kakugi [martial skills] in the field of combat sports.

In these hard times my father, Kisshomaru the second Doshu, made remarkable achievements in supporting my grandfather, the Founder, saving aikido from the ruins of the wartime fire and finally leading it to the present prosperity. So far as the position of the Chief Director is concerned, my father held the office for thirty years since 1967, but my father, the second Doshu, substantially bore the heaviest responsibility for fifty years after the war.

As the present Doshu and Director I ask myself what I can do, what I should do. My conclusion is that all I can and should do

The author together with his family at the party for celebrating his reception of a Blue Ribbon Medal; the front row from the right: the author with Tomoteru, Mitsuteru's second son, his wife, Kyoko, and Hiroteru, Mitsuteru's first son; the second row from the right: Sachiko, the author's first daughter, Mitsuteru, his first son, and Keiko, Mitsuteru's wife

is to take a natural attitude to everything and try to realize 'wa [harmony]', which is the essence of aikido. What I need to do, in other words, is to take care that we should not disturb the tradition of 'wa', which the Founder created and the second Doshu spread to the world, and pass the present order down to the next generation. In so doing, I also have to listen to young people of the new generation, whose opinions are totally different from those of young people living before and right after the war.

One of the important things in operating our organization is to make a clear distinction between what should be changed and

The author visiting the Tsurugaoka Hachiman Shrine in Kamakura prior to his annual dedicatory performance and lesson at the training hall in its precinct in May

what should not be changed. It is often pointed out today that values have been diversified. We have a variety of choices even in the field of hobbies and learning activities. Martial arts also should not keep aloof from the general trend of diversification in our times. On the other hand, it would be almost unthinkable to be subservient in going along with the current of the times. Those people who have chosen martial arts out of many options are presumably expecting to learn something unique to them. This is reasonably inferred when we look at the way foreign students of aikido expect to attain something they cannot find in their cultures. What I intend to do is to keep what should not be changed—the essence of aikido—as it is and at the same time to provide suitable environments for present-day trainees.

I ask myself another question: how can aikido be a 'modern martial art' in the true sense of the word? My conclusion is that it is truly a modern martial art and a martial art of the twenty-first century as it is with its traditional principles: it has no contest, can be practiced by almost everyone regardless of age and sex, and makes it possible for us to train ourselves physically as well as spiritually with its deep philosophy of *aiki* [spiritual harmony]. We cannot and need not change these principles. Then, again, what should I do? I think it is to provide and improve training environments not only in Japan but all also in foreign countries.

Now that the circle of aikido has expanded to the world, as Doshu at the centre of the circle, I intend to consistently and carefully convey the 'spirit' of aikido, which is the very basis of training. I truly hope that aikido will shine out as the 'silver bridge' that the Founder imagined.

March 2018

Brief Personal Records
of Successive Doshus

Morihei Ueshiba (1883-1969)

1883 Born in Nishinotani Village, Nishimuro County, Wakayama Prefecture (now Uenoyama, Tanabe City, Wakayama Prefecture) on December the 14th.

1908 Got a license of jujutsu of the Yagyu-shingan school from Masanosuke Tsuboi.

1911 Responded to the government's policy of inviting cultivating groups to Hokkaido and migrated the next year to Shirataki-genya, Monbetsu County, Hokkaido, as the leader of the group of developers consisting of fifty-four families. Received instruction in jujutsu of the Daito school from Sokaku Takeda.

1919 Received the news of his father becoming critically ill and left for his home. Made a stopover at Ayabe-cho, Kyoto Prefecture, on the way and met Onisaburo Deguchi of the religious sect of Oomoto and was fascinated by him. Moved to Ayabe, Kyoto with his family after his father's death and established a training dojo called 'Ueshiba Juku'.

1926 Founded a new type of budo, which he called 'Aiki-no-michi [the Way of Aiki]'.

1927 Moved to Tokyo with his family and gave martial instruction at many institutes including the Naval Academy.

1931 Established a dojo specializing in aikido training in Ushigomewakamatsu-cho (now Wakamatsu-cho in the Shinjuku ward).

1940 Had the dojo authorized to become a juridical foundation.

1941 Established an out-door dojo in Iwama-cho, Ibaraki Prefecture.

1955 Devoted himself to the promotion of aikido inside and outside Japan.

1960 Received a Purple Ribbon Medal for his achievement of founding aikido.

1964 Was decorated the Fourth Order of the Rizing Sun, Gold Rays with Rosette.

1969 Died on April the 26th at the age of eighty-six and was conferred the Third Order of the Sacred Treasure (Senior Grade of the Fifth Court Rank) in honour of his achievements in founding and promoting aikido.

Kisshomaru Ueshiba (1921-1999)

1921 Born on June 27th as the third son of Morihei Ueshiba, the Founder of aikido.

1946 Graduated from the School of Political Science and Economics, Waseda University.

1948 Became the Director of the Hombu Dojo of Aikido in place of the Founder.

1967 Took office as the Chief Director of the Aikikai Foundation.

1969 Succeeded to the position of Doshu owing to the Founder's death.

1986 Was conferred a Blue Ribbon Medal for his achievements in promoting aikido.

1995 Was conferred the Third Order of the Sacred Treasure.

1996 Filled many important posts including the President of the International Aikido Federation, President of the Japan Students' Association of Aikido, and Director of the Nippon Budokan Foundation.

1999 Died on January 4th and was conferred the Senior Grade of the Fifth Court Rank by the Japanese government.

Moriteru Ueshiba (1951-)

1951 Born on April 2nd as the second son of Kisshomaru Ueshiba the second Doshu of aikido.

1976 Graduated from the Faculty of Economics, Meiji Gakuin University.

1985 Took office as Managing Director.

1986 Took office as Director of the Hombu Dojo of Aikido.

1996 Took office as Chief Director of the Aikikai Federation.

1999 Succeeded to the position of Doshu owing to the second Doshu's death.

2004 Took office as special lecturer at Tohoku University.

2006 Received an Anchieta Medal of Brazil. Became emeritus visiting professor at International Budo University.

2009 Was awarded the Order of Friendship from the Russian Federation.

2010 Took office as special invited professor at Kogakkan University (till 2017).

2012 Took office as Chief Director of the Aikikai Public Utility Foundation owing to the change of status of Aikikai from an incorporated foundation to public utility foundation. Received the Gold Medal from University of Valencia.

2013 Was conferred a Blue Ribbon Medal for his achievements of publicizing and promoting aikido. Filled many important posts including the Director of the Nippon Budokan Public Utility Foundation and Senator at International Budo University.

英訳————斎藤兆史
装幀————ゴトウアキヒロ

Aikido, the Contemporary Martial Art of Harmony:
Training Methods and Spiritual Teachings

英訳版　合気道　稽古とこころ

現代に生きる調和の武道

発行日	2019 年　9 月 30 日　第 1 刷
著　者	植芝守央
発行者	清田名人
発行所	株式会社内外出版社
	〒 110-8578 東京都台東区東上野 2-1-11
	電話　03-5830-0368　（企画販売局）
	電話　03-5830-0237　（編集部）
	https://www.naigai-p.co.jp
印刷・製本	中央精版印刷株式会社

ISBN 978-4-86257-472-5　C0075